CHANGE YOUR FREQUENCY
CHANGE YOUR DESTINY

THE SCIENCE OF PROSPERITY

DAVID WONG

QI LIFE

DISCLAIMER

"Frequency is the code that creates and shapes our reality." — *David Wong*

CONTENTS

CHANGE YOUR FREQUENCY
CHANGE YOUR DESTINY

INTRODUCTION

Every thought you hold has the power to change your reality. Each moment, every choice, offers a new opportunity to mold the world to your will. Imagine you hold a remote control that can tune the world around you as you please. I want you to think of a place where success isn't just a fleeting idea, but a constant, tangible state that you can summon at will. Now, picture yourself in a world where healing goes beyond mere possibility, becoming a daily reality. Does this world seem possible to you? Are you able to visualize it clearly? Does it feel like something attainable *for you*?

If these ideas stir something within you—if they paint a picture as vivid and tangible as anything you've seen—then you've picked up the right book at exactly the right moment. This book is meant for you. You're exactly the person these words were written for.

You may be sitting there, book in hand, feeling disconnected or perhaps even at odds with the universe. Maybe you feel like the different aspects of your life are out of alignment, leaving you feeling disharmonious and out of tune. Or maybe things are going well for you—life is good, or even great—but there's a gnawing feeling inside you that something vital is missing. You're seeking something more, something that can push your life from good to truly extraordinary.

This book speaks directly to you. Our minds and bodies are intricate instruments that can be tuned to achieve a state of higher harmony and potential. Just as a finely tuned instrument can produce sublime music, so too can your life, when tuned to the right frequencies, resonate with the music of success and fulfillment.

As the founder of Qi Life, I've spearheaded the integration of age-old wisdom with modern technology to unlock doors that many don't even realize exist. In your journey through this book, you'll uncover the hidden potential of frequency technology through the powerful stories of those who have already experienced its transformative effects.

Imagine the story of a real estate agent who woke up to a day like any other, but by its close, she was $90,000 richer. After applying the principles outlined in this guide, she tapped into a frequency specifically attuned to attract wealth and opportunity. Almost like magic, her client list grew exponentially, culminating in a deal that earned her an unexpected and life-changing commission. This wasn't just a stroke of good luck; it was a direct result of aligning her personal frequency with that of abundance and success.

Then consider a Paralympic athlete, whose limitations seemed to define his capabilities. Frustrated with his progress and recovery times, he turned to frequency therapy, hoping for a small improvement. What he found was nothing short of miraculous. The right frequencies not only hastened his recovery but also boosted his performance, allowing him to surpass his own expectations and achieve new personal bests. His story is a testament to the fact that our bodies and abilities are not fixed but are capable of extraordinary change when tuned correctly.

Among these narratives is also that of a singer, who had long harboured a dream of collaborating with a specific musician—a name she had written down years ago on her vision board. Despite her talent, anxiety and self-doubt clouded her path. That was until she discovered the power of abundance frequencies. Shortly after starting her journey with these frequencies, a chance encounter led to the collaboration of her dreams. More than just a professional triumph, this experience marked a significant personal victory over the anxiety that had once held her back.

These stories are just glimpses of what's possible when you harness the correct frequencies. They are real-life examples of ordinary people achieving extraordinary results, not through luck or coincidence, but through a deliberate enhancement of their life's frequencies. This book is your guide to understanding how you can achieve similar, if not greater, successes in your own life. Whether you seek healing, abundance, or personal growth, the keys to unlocking these doors lie within the pages ahead.

As you continue reading, remember that these experiences, as incredible as they seem, are within your reach. The journey of transformation that began for these individuals can just as easily begin for you today. Why continue to dream of a better life when the means to achieve it are waiting for you? Let's explore together how the subtle but powerful adjustment of your frequencies can open up a world of possibilities.

Allow me to introduce myself. My name is David Wong, also known as The Frequency Expert. I'm a health-tech founder, bestselling author, inventor, musician, martial artist, and entrepreneur. My mission—and that of Qi Life—is to elevate the planet's frequency, to usher in an era of unprecedented healing and abundance. This mission might seem lofty, but as you delve deeper into this book, you'll understand that it's not just achievable; it's essential. We are not merely made to exist; we are designed to thrive, to resonate with the universe in a harmony that brings forth our highest potentials.

In the beginning, the universe itself was spoken into existence. "Let there be light," and light there was. This ancient verse from Genesis encapsulates the profound truth that intention, coupled with utterance, is the precursor to creation. This principle is our foundation as we delve into the transformative power of frequency.

Across various cultures and beliefs, the narrative is consistent: deities shaped the cosmos by manipulating energy according to their divine will. If we, made in the image of such power, inherit these capabilities, isn't it our sacred duty to also shape our world? This book challenges you to embrace that duty—not just as a passive observer of your life but as an active participant in its creation.

You might wonder how this is relevant in a modern context, where society often values incremental, conventional paths to success. These traditional paths, however, frequently lead to dead ends. But once you grasp the ancient wisdom of energy and frequency, as well as their application through modern technology, you will view your potential through a new lens.

As you turn each page, you'll encounter more stories, more insights, and the scientific breakthroughs behind them. You'll see how adjusting your own frequency can change your health, wealth, and personal growth. You'll learn how to tap into frequencies that can transform the mundane into the miraculous.

If you put this book down now, you risk missing out on the foundational knowledge that could revolutionize your life. You'll miss out on the techniques that have transformed lives and the insights that can propel you to live the life you've always dreamed of.

So, I invite you to continue. Turn the page. Embark on this journey of discovery and transformation with me. Let's explore together how the power of frequency can not only change your life but also contribute to the profound healing and advancement of our world. This is just the beginning...

CHAPTER 1

THE FREQUENCY MINDSET

L et's talk about something interesting: energy fields! They might be invisible but they are literally all around you. To really tap into them, start thinking in terms of frequencies. This is where your transformation and self-discovery kick off. The idea of a *"frequency mindset"* might sound a bit out there, but hang tight. In this first chapter, we're going to break it down so you can really get a handle on it. Embracing this mindset is how you'll gain the tools and insights you need to change the way you see and move through the world.

The first thing we need to tackle is what we mean by 'frequency'. Simply put, a frequency is the specific channel or waveband used to send signals. It tells us how often a vibration happens within a second. Pretty much everything in the universe, whether it's alive or not, gives off some kind of vibrational frequency. What you see, hear, and feel around you is all down to these frequencies being picked up and decoded by your brain and senses.

There are roughly eighty-six billion active neurons in your brain (Saladin, 2011; von Bartheld, 2016). These tiny nerve cells, or neurons, are pretty amazing. They pick up, process, and send out electrical signals, forming connections known as synapses. It's these networks of synapses that let us see, feel, touch, and think. Basically, they make everything we do, experience, and even dream of achieving—whether it's mental, physical, or spiritual—possible. And all this happens thanks to electrical currents, or energy, flowing through our brains. It's like our own personal power grid!

Our brains *process* things faster than our senses can keep up, especially when it comes to seeing and hearing. Believe it or not, your brain catches on to what's happening around you quicker than you might realize. MIT neuroscientists found something profound: the brain can recognize what the eyes see in just thirteen milliseconds. In experiments, when people were shown images quickly one after another, their brains picked up on the images up to twenty times faster than their eyes did. So, in a way, your brain is 'seeing' faster than your eyes. This makes sense because there's always a tiny delay—a lag—between seeing something and understanding it. Your eyes see it, then the optic nerves have to send this information to your brain, which then has to figure it all out. So technically, we're all living a few microseconds in the past. What this MIT study shows is that during this lag, our brains are actually doing a lot more than we thought. The brain is processing the data for its own use before making it available for your conscious interpretation and reaction (Trafton, 2014; Markowsky). This research tells us something pretty intriguing: there are hidden neural pathways in our brains, kind of like undercover energy centres. These are buzzing away behind the scenes, influencing us in ways we don't even notice.

The ancient Chinese had a term for this: "Yi" (意). They believed in "three mind centres" or "Three Dantians"—focus flow centres of energy crucial for meditative exercises like martial arts and qigong (Yang, 1989; Cohen, 1999). These centres, filled with what they called 'life force' or 'qi,' are linked to our basic instincts and self-preservation capabilities (Paul, 1987).

The Upper Dantian, located in the forehead near the eyebrows, is tied to spiritual awareness and intuition, impacting mental and psychic abilities. The Middle Dantian, found in the chest near the heart, manages emotions and is connected to feelings like love, joy, and compassion. It also helps distribute energy throughout the body. The Lower Dantian, in the lower belly, stores and builds Qi. It's essential for physical health and energy, helping keep the practitioner stable and centred.

In essence, ancient teachings suggest that we all possess hidden energy forces within us. These energies, although not part of our everyday awareness, can be accessed and harnessed with the right approach.

It makes sense that if the cells in our bodies use electrical signals to communicate, they could be influenced by external frequencies. This could allow our brains and bodies to adapt, heal in new ways, experience different states of consciousness, and even change how we fundamentally operate. This process is known as 'neural programming,' thanks to something called neuroplasticity, which I'll talk about later.

In simpler terms, 'frequency' in your daily life means the vibrations and electromagnetic energies that come from your thoughts and emotions. Picture your mind and heart sending out unique energy signals, like notes in a symphony that create the soundtrack of your life. These frequencies mold your experiences, relationships, and what happens to you. Every thought and emotion you have sends out its own wave frequency.

The term 'emotion' comes from the Latin word *emotere*, meaning 'energy in motion'. Researcher and psychiatrist David R. Hawkins is known for having created a scale to measure the energy levels in our consciousness across different emotions. When you feel an emotion, your body and brain turn its frequency into physical sensations. According to the Law of Conservation of Energy, energy isn't created or destroyed; it just changes form. For example, think about the last time you were angry and felt physically hot—that's an emotion's energy transforming. Understanding this, it's clear how we can change the energies we experience through our emotions.

Quantum physics has shown us that every frequency, with its unique peaks and valleys in wave form, can be altered or manipulated. These wave shapes act as encoders and decoders of information and data. Today's cutting-edge science is all about how we can change this information and data, not just through external influences, but by our own internal will—our choices and intentions.

Think back to a time when you felt truly alive, confident, and full of joy. In that moment, your frequency was high, filled with positivity, radiating positivity and attracting favourable circumstances. On the flip side, during moments of doubt, fear, or negativity, your frequency probably dropped, leading to less favourable experiences and a tougher reality.

The notion of changing your thoughts or emotions might seem complex, but it's something we've been encouraged to do all our lives. Think about how often you've heard phrases like "think positive" or "be the change you want to see." These sayings are so common that we often overlook them. Sometimes, they might even annoy us because we know there's truth in them. Like it or not, we need to understand how our thoughts and feelings, on a subatomic level, affect our daily lives. Every day, our brains process over 60,000 thoughts and emotions. If you can spot the negative ones and let them go, you can start to control how you see the world, and thus, the world you experience. Recognizing your emotions as shifts in energy frequencies inside you lets you *choose* which emotions to feel and experience.

Even a basic look at words can be enlightening. Take the word 'stress'—what feelings does it stir up in you? What parts of your life come to mind? Now, switch to the word 'relax'. How does that change your mood? Does it calm the stressful thoughts you had just moments ago? This is a straightforward example of balancing your thoughts through the power of words.

To change your thinking, you first need to realize that it's your perception of the world that shapes your reality. This means you can't just coast on autopilot—you have to actively *choose* how you see things. By doing this, you're constantly fine-tuning the frequencies of your mind (your cognitive perception) and your heart (your spiritual perception). You have a lot more control over what goes on inside you than what happens around you. So, by starting internally, you can better align yourself with the external world you want to build throughout your life. This approach is what we call the frequency mindset, and it's key to fundamentally transforming your life.

I like to break down the process of manifestation into three steps:

1. **Visualize:** *clearly* envision your goal
2. **Resonate:** *really* feel the emotions of your goal already having been achieved or attained
3. **Amplify:** *augment* your resonance by incorporating external energy / frequency stimuli

Let's discuss each step…

When *visualizing,* start by clearly defining your goal. What is it that you want to acquire, achieve, or experience? Visualization is like creating a mini version of your goal in the universe—you simulate its energy or frequency. Although it might just be a thought in the vast universe, by perceiving it, you make it real, at least to your senses. Remember, everything you see started as someone's vision. Take the example of a new sports car: imagine yourself in the driver's seat. Feel the steering wheel under your hands, touch the dashboard and the leather upholstery, smell the new-car-scent, and listen to the engine or the stereo. Engage all your senses to experience every detail of the car as if it were real. This full sensory immersion makes your visualization powerful and vivid.

In the *resonating* step, you allow your goal to expand within your imagination. Experience the emotions you'd feel upon achieving it—

joy, excitement, a sense of accomplishment, satisfaction, and content-ment. Imagine your heart is full, you're soaring high, and you feel unstoppable. Feeling these emotions deeply sets the emotional ground-work that can help turn your goal into reality. Remember, the term 'emotion' means *energy in motion*. Your emotions are crucial for mani-festing what you desire. They not only carry your feelings; they *are* energy. Recognizing your emotions as tools rather than mere reactions to experiences lets you *use them* strategically to push forward, evolve, and grow. Emotional theorist and researcher Barbara Fredrickson describes emotional energy as functioning on either an upward, expanding spiral, or a downward, contracting one (Garland, 2010). Which kind do you feel is usually flowing through *you*? Did you know that your brain reacts more quickly to emotions than to analytical thinking? The areas of your brain that handle emotions are better connected than those that process analytical data. Moreover, when it comes to basic survival instincts, feelings like stress, fear, and worry often overshadow feelings of happiness and peace. This insight is quite revealing about how our brains prioritize and respond to different stimuli. It teaches us that consciously resonating in and prioritizing our positive emotions can improve our well-being and therefore our ability to manifest positive outcomes in our lives (Schwartz, 2002; Goleman, 1995; LeDoux, 1992). And if you can resonate in positivity, you can amplify it, too…

In the *amplification* step, you immerse yourself in the frequencies and energies needed to actualize your goal. Sometimes, visualizing and resonating alone are enough to generate the internal energy or frequency needed to move towards your goal. However, incorporating external energies can often accelerate and refine the process. Properly aligning with external frequencies can even automate parts of the manifestation process. This is what we refer to as energy alignment—it helps synchronize your internal goals with the external world to achieve them more effectively.

Oftentimes, people get stuck in the visualizing or resonating phases. They can imagine their goals and feel the emotions of achieving them, but if their frequencies aren't properly aligned, they struggle to make these goals a reality. This blockage can happen for various reasons, but it's usually because they haven't released the negative emotions and frequencies that hold them back. Emotions like fear, self-doubt, and embarrassment can be significant obstacles. Additionally, we're continuously bombarded with negative frequencies— from media, news, other people, and even the technology we use, like Wi-Fi and 5G. These pervasive energies can create a subtly negative environment at home, work, or in public, which might hold you back without your conscious awareness. Recognizing and addressing these influences is crucial for moving forward and achieving your goals.

By leveraging technologies like those developed by Qi Life, you can effectively synchronize your cognitive (brain) and spiritual (heart) frequencies. This allows you to tap into positive external energy sources, whether they're the natural frequencies around you or digital simulations. This is the essence of the *amplification* step—enhancing what the universe already provides. Using this technology can automate the process, encouraging your mind and body to resonate with an exponential increase of positive energy. This alignment ensures that your perceptions and reality consistently match the outcomes you desire and the goals you aim to achieve.

Albert Einstein is believed to have said, "The world as we have created it is a process of our thinking. It cannot be changed without changing our thinking. No problem can be solved from the same level of consciousness that created it. We must learn to see the world anew." This means that to really engage with the frequency mindset, you need to master the art of steering your perceptions and reactions. Adjusting how you perceive and respond to your environment is key to transforming your experience and the world around you.

Perception is your interpretation of events or occurrences—it's how you make sense of what happens to you. Every event triggers a thought, feeling, or emotion, followed by some kind of response. Often, our first reaction to an event can be unexpected, and negative thoughts or emotions may even come as a surprise to ourselves. While your initial reaction may be involuntary, how you choose to respond is completely within your control. In essence, *perception* is about interpretation, and your *response* is your reaction. The way you respond can either correct a negative frequency or continue it. Adopting a frequency mindset allows you to navigate the world more effectively, tuning the energy around you to better meet your needs and desires. This approach doesn't just help manage challenges; it actively reshapes your environment to support your goals.

One of the most effective strategies you can employ is to ask the right questions whenever you face obstacles. Shift your perspective from victimhood to empowerment by changing the nature of your inquiries:

- Instead of asking, "*Why is this happening to me?*" ask, "*How can this benefit me?*"
- Instead of looking for someone to blame, ask, "*How can I take responsibility in this moment?*"
- Instead of dwelling on what went wrong, consider, "*What positive outcome can arise from this?*"

By transforming how you approach these moments of challenge, you turn negative energy into an opportunity that aligns with your vision for yourself. This proactive approach is a key part of maintaining a frequency mindset and navigating life's ups and downs effectively.

While adapting to this mindset can be challenging, much of the difficulty stems from our brains' tendency to prioritize comfort over challenge. Our perception of the present is largely shaped by our past experiences, not our future aspirations. This reliance on familiarity helps in daily tasks, like dressing or making a sandwich, because it saves us from having to relearn these actions every day. However, it also creates a comfort zone that can dull our engagement with the present and future, making us content with the familiar rather than inspired to seek out new challenges.

Adopting a frequency mindset empowers you to interact with the present more actively. By tuning into the energy waveforms around you, you can intuit future possibilities more clearly, moving away from being solely influenced by past experiences. Regularly evaluating how you interpret events enables you to respond more effectively to current situations. The key is recognizing and accepting that you control your destiny. Your perceptions shape your behaviours, and your behaviours dictate your actions. By managing your *internal* world, you can influence your *external* world. Shift away from negativity, self-doubt, and fear, and embrace confidence, optimism, and gratitude. **Change your frequency, and you change your destiny.**

Once you've mastered this skill set, a transformative shift will occur in your life. You'll experience a profound restructuring of your mind, heart, and spirit. Opportunities that were once invisible will suddenly become clear. Strained relationships will heal and grow stronger. Your life will be infused with a fresh vibrancy, full of possibility and opportunity. Even if you've never considered or practiced it before, *you* have the power to change your reality by simply adjusting your frequency.

Ultimately, adopting a *frequency mindset* is about embracing growth and empowerment. It allows you to break free from the cycle of repetitive experiences and unlock your true potential. Remember, your perception shapes your reality.

I know this to be true from my own personal experience. This book isn't about me, but by sharing a bit of my own story, I hope to show how adopting a frequency mindset can be a game-changer in your life, too. My own path began in childhood with a near-death experience at the age of nine, after a fall from a three-story balcony at school. I sustained multiple injuries, including a fractured skull, and the lengthy recovery changed me. I shifted from being an extrovert to becoming more introverted and reserved. It was during this period that my brother introduced me to spiritual pursuits, which led me to discover the power of music and frequencies. This new interest in energy and soundwaves opened a door to martial arts, where I embraced wing chun, tai chi, and qigong—further exploring the flow of energy through the body. These experiences were crucial in shaping the person I am today and in developing the frequency mindset that has transformed my life.

Even though I immersed myself in spiritual and physical practices throughout my formative years, I still faced ongoing challenges with depression, chronic fatigue, and brain fog. I also struggled with a severe, incurable digestive disease which caused such intense internal bleeding that I often couldn't leave the house. Despite consulting medical experts, the condition was deemed 'incurable'. Pharmaceutical treatments failed to help and often led to additional issues like eczema, which made me abandon them. I also tried naturopathic approaches, including acupuncture and various traditional Chinese remedies. These methods only slightly eased my symptoms and were costly, draining hundreds of dollars each month. Looking back, I often wonder how I managed to endure those years of suffering. It became clear to me that it was my dedication to qigong, along with prayer and meditation, that sustained me. These practices didn't cure me but kept me going, maintaining a sense of survival against the odds.

Dealing with my health issues alongside cognitive impairments created relentless cycles of highs and lows in my life. This instability took a heavy toll on my ability to achieve what I wanted. I saw personal and professional relationships fall apart, lost jobs, and watched as my investments—both time and resources—evaporated. Finally, I hit rock bottom: a day when I was literally drained of life from all the bleeding, broke, lonely, and frustrated at my lack of progress toward my dreams over the previous decade. In that moment of despair, I broke down and cried out to God, "What do you want me to do to get out of this? Just tell me what to do, and I will do it." In the quiet that followed, while I prostrated with my head to the ground, a small voice answered, "David, meditate." Shocked yet intrigued by this response, I began to deeply explore the art and science of meditation from that day forward.

Naturally, my interest in meditation gravitated towards using music, sound, frequency, and energy—areas I had been exploring and developing since my younger years. It was thrilling to discover that these skills, which had long been part of my life, could also be harnessed to aid in my healing process.

In my research, I noticed a common thread among the great ancient civilizations—the Egyptians, Mesopotamians, Mayans, Aztecs, and others. They all had a clear understanding of the body's energy. They left behind evidence of their practices focusing on vibrational energy, which we commonly refer to today as frequency. Each civilization recognized and harnessed this energy in their own unique ways.

Consider the ancient Greeks, for example, where figures like King Pyrrhus were said to heal people using an invisible energy force. Similarly, the Egyptians wrote of an energy sourced from the star system Sirius, known as 'sekhem'. The Bible also includes examples of energy healing, many performed by Jesus himself. In Japan, this concept is referred to as 'reiki' or 'universal energy', used for physical and emotional recovery and development. Reiki traces its origins back to even older energy practices found in ancient Chinese culture, referred to as 'qi' or qi energy. This energy is believed to be manipulable within the body to enhance various cognitive and physical functions. The formal practice of manipulating qi energy is called qigong. "When the flow of qi is impaired, we have disease. When it flows easily, we have perfect health." These are the words of Master Hong Liu (Liu, 1997). What all these ancient traditions of energy and frequency share is the belief that their respective energy forces are interconnected with everything in the universe. This concept, once seen as purely spiritual or mystical, is now increasingly recognized by science as being grounded in reality. These traditions understood that the energy flowing within us is part of a much larger, universal network of energy.

In 1952, renowned German physicist Winfried Otto Schumann identified that the Earth generates a resonant frequency of 7.83 Hz (Montiel, 2005). This discovery is significant because it closely aligns with the frequency at which our brain's alpha waves resonate. (Foster,

2017) I'll talk more about this in Chapter Two, but for now, it's important to note that this frequency serves as a background energy field influencing our biological circuitry (Dispenza, 2019).

This exploration led me to discover forms of meditation that utilize specific frequencies. As I practiced these techniques, I was amazed by their profound impact on my body and emotions—it was truly transformative. The more I learned and applied these principles, the better I understood the energy fields around me. This knowledge empowered me to control these fields, to fine-tune them, which brought me an unprecedented clarity. It felt as though all the blockages in my psyche and personality were being cleared. My depression lifted, my mood improved dramatically, and I could achieve specific emotional states almost on demand. Whether I needed focus or motivation, I learned to harness the necessary energy instantly and effortlessly. This journey showed me that *energy is controllable* and can also be a powerful tool for personal transformation.

I realized that my experiences with meditation were pretty unique. I was actually creating the life I wanted, but achieving this deep state of mind through meditation isn't something everyone can easily do. Most people just don't have the time or effort required to develop meditative expertise. I started thinking about how I could help others reach this deep connection between their heart, body, and mind, and achieve real benefits like motivation and success. At the heart of my own meditation was something simple yet powerful: energy frequencies. So, I thought, why not create specific frequencies that could help others in the same way they helped me? With this idea, I teamed up with top scientists in the field. Together, we developed our own unique frequencies. This effort led to the creation of Qi Life, a company that offers these frequencies to help people transform their lives.

From the start, our aim was to develop the ultimate frequency therapy system—a mix of frequencies, technology, devices, and resources that would change the way people interact with frequency in their daily lives. We wanted to make it modern, accessible, and user-friendly. This wasn't an easy task, and there was plenty of skepticism at the beginning, even from me. Although there were older types of equipment from as far back as the 1930s that some people had found success with, I was determined to push beyond the existing boundaries.

The more time I spend working in this field, the more I realize how transformative this technology can be. I'm not just a developer or an inventor—I'm also a user, and a true believer. I've seen the effects first-hand. Using this technology has not only transformed my own life, but it continues to transform me daily. I like to say that our technology can improve our users' lives by 1% each and every day. I'm reminded of the words of Pranic healing master Tirumalai Krishnamacharya, often called the 'father of modern yoga,' whose insights have deeply influenced my understanding of personal growth and healing. He is quoted as saying, "Think of God. If not God, the sun. If not the sun, your parents" (Pagés Ruiz, 2001). In simple terms, energy connects *everything*. It's the foundation of our lives, our realities, and our dreams. The frequency mindset is all about using this fundamental building block to transform our lives. I can say with certainty that adopting this mindset has changed my life, and I believe it can change yours as well.

Now that we've introduced the frequency mindset, let's look ahead at what we'll explore together. The upcoming chapters are designed to show how your thoughts, emotions, and meditative practices not only affect your mental and emotional health but also the physiology of your brain and body. More importantly, we'll dive into how frequency technology can automate, amplify, and accelerate your journey of self-transformation. This technology works without requiring much time, willpower, or even conscious effort from you—no need for extensive knowledge, training, or conscious participation.

Throughout this book, we'll explore the science behind these profound transformations. We'll delve into practical techniques and systems that empower you to harness the frequency mindset as a tool for personal growth, healing, and achieving abundance. My goal is to give you a comprehensive understanding of how your frequency impacts every aspect of your life and to provide you with the tools to actively shape your reality going forward.

As we dig deeper, remember that the power to change your life is firmly in your hands. The frequency mindset is your key to unlocking the vast potential within you. Let's explore how it can shape your destiny...

CHAPTER 2
THE SCIENCE OF FREQUENCY

As we embark on our journey to understand the frequency mindset, it's important to first establish a strong foundation rooted in science. In this chapter, we'll dive into how thoughts and emotions can influence brain activity and shape our neural pathways. We'll also examine the transformative power of neuroplasticity and the critical role of brainwave frequencies, all supported by robust scientific research. This foundation will help us appreciate the deep connections between our mental processes and their physical manifestations.

THOUGHTS AND EMOTIONS SHAPE YOUR BRAIN

Thoughts and emotions significantly influence brain activity. Neuroscientists have extensively studied this relationship, finding that our mental and emotional states initiate complex electrical and chemical signalling patterns in the brain. For example, experiencing negative emotions such as fear or stress activate specific neural pathways. On the other hand, positive emotions like love and gratitude stimulate different areas of the brain, enhancing our overall well-being. These insights help us understand the powerful connection between our emotional experiences and brain function.

As discussed in Chapter One, emotions carry their own frequencies that can extend beyond our physiological boundaries and impact the external realities of our lives. A particularly intriguing study that highlights this concept involved a group of nuns in the 1930s. The Mother Superior asked each nun to write her autobiography. Decades later, in the 1990s, researcher David Snowdon and his team at the University of Kentucky analyzed these autobiographies. They coded each word related to emotional experiences as positive, negative, or neutral and counted their occurrences. Remarkably, they discovered that the nuns who used more positive words in their writings were more likely to be alive sixty years later. This study suggests a powerful link between positive emotional expression and longevity (Davidson, 2012). But how exactly do emotions influence our lifespan? As we've explored, emotions generate specific frequencies that are transmitted through neural signals within the body. These thoughts and emotions directly affect your brain's activity, which then impact your body either positively or negatively. Essentially, a positive mindset contributes to a healthier body, and this combination can naturally lead to a longer lifespan. The way our emotions shape our physiological responses illustrates the profound connection between mind, body, and overall well-being.

Nuns, like many people of faith, regularly engage in prayer, which is essentially a form of meditation. Prayer involves actively choosing to be grateful and thankful, and it's one of the most effective ways to cultivate a frequency mindset. As Ralph Waldo Emerson poignantly stated, "Sow a thought and you reap an action; sow an act and you reap a habit; sow a habit and you reap a character; sow a character and you reap a destiny." Essentially, our destiny is shaped by our thoughts and feelings, a notion echoed in religious texts worldwide.

For instance, in Philippians 4:8, the Bible encourages, "Finally, brothers and sisters, whatever is true, whatever is noble, whatever is right, whatever is pure, whatever is lovely, whatever is admirable—if anything is excellent or praiseworthy—think about such things." By focusing on these positive thoughts, by *thinking of such things*, we begin to manifest them, turning them into habits, as Emerson suggested. I will explore this concept further later, but first, let's examine another study that highlights the transformative power of deep thought and meditation.

Led by Richard Davidson, a renowned neuroscientist and professor at the University of Wisconsin-Madison, this study illustrated the profound impact of meditation on the brain. Utilizing brain scans and neuroimaging techniques, Davidson and his team discovered that regular meditation can lead to significant changes in brain structure, especially in areas related to emotional regulation and empathy. They observed that meditation boosts electromagnetic activity in brain regions involved in decision-making and focused attention tasks (Davidson, 2003). This research underscores how meditation not only affects our mental state but physically molds our brain to enhance functions critical for a balanced and empathetic life.

Davidson and his team compared the neural activity of meditation beginners with that of experienced meditators. Both groups underwent magnetic resonance imaging (MRI) scans while engaging in medita-tion. The findings revealed that those with more meditation experience showed increased activation in their brain circuits, enhancing their ability to concentrate and remain focused on tasks. Davidson noted, "We found that regions of the brain that are intimately involved in the control and regulation of attention, such as the prefrontal cortex, were more activated in the long-term practitioners." This indicates that meditative experience not only makes concentration more effortless but also demonstrates that managing your thoughts and emotions can significantly influence your brain activity. Davidson insists that "Atten-tion can be trained, and in a way that is not fundamentally different from how physical exercise changes the body." (Tenenbaum, 2007). We hear so often that the brain is a muscle and needs to be worked out like the body, and it's true.

This groundbreaking research highlights the dynamic connection between our inner world of thoughts and emotions and the physical structures of our brain. Researchers like Davidson suggest that through neural therapies, it's possible to alter undesirable brain functions, such as a negative outlook or impaired concentration. The term for this transformative effect on the brain is 'neuroplasticity'. This concept underscores the brain's remarkable ability to adapt and change in response to our mental activities, proving that our mental states can reshape our neurological pathways.

NEUROPLASTICITY: REWIRING THE BRAIN THROUGH MEDITATION AND POSITIVE THINKING

Neuroplasticity is a concept that Davidson has been equally involved in over the years. In a nutshell, neuroplasticity is the theory that the "the brain is neither immutable nor static but continuously remodelled by the lives we lead" (Radler, 2012). In other words, the brain has an incredible ability to rewire itself based on experiences and deliberate practices, or habits. Research and natural human experiences have both contributed greatly to our understanding of this phenomenon. For example, individuals who have suffered a stroke or those who are blind or deaf have demonstrated that damage to one part of the brain can lead to increased activity in other parts, compensating for the loss. This finding has been a groundbreaking revelation in neuroscience, significantly altering our understanding of the brain's capacity for change. It shows us that through intentional practices like meditation, mindfulness, and positive thinking, we can actively reshape our neural pathways, much like the brain naturally adjusts in response to physical impairments.

It was once believed that emotions disrupted cognitive processes, but research into neuroplasticity has shown that emotions are actually adaptive, not disruptive. Emotions play a crucial role in higher brain functions such as decision-making and behaviour. Therefore, to lead a better life, it's important to embrace and utilize the influence of our emotions. Davidson's research made this clear. "An honest systematic observation, I think, will convince anyone that [...] complex decisions require that we consult with our emotions" (Winerman, 2012). Davidson identified six 'Emotional Styles' that explain how our emotions influence brain activity and, consequently, how we navigate our lives. These styles help us understand the specific ways emotions shape our daily interactions and decisions.

1. **Resilience:** the rate at which we overcome adverse scenarios
2. **Outlook:** the length of time positive emotions persist
3. **Intuition:** the accuracy of our ability to decode non-verbal signals
4. **Self-Awareness:** the accuracy with which we decode our own bodily cues related to emotion (heart rate, sweating, muscle tension, etcetera)
5. **Context:** our sensitivity to contextual input and how we respond
6. **Attention:** our ability to be influenced or to resist environmental emotional stimuli

Our brain circuitry, which includes the electrical energy or frequencies, supports various 'Emotional Styles' that dictate how our brains function. Depending on the style, you can actively train or adjust them using your conscious will. For instance, if you tend to have a negative outlook, you might want to shift this aspect of your perception to enhance positivity. Similarly, if your contextual style impedes appropriate emotional responses to your environment, addressing this can lead to better interactions. Davidson emphasizes the importance of the 'Resilience Style' as a crucial determinant in one's ability to lead a fulfilling life. He notes, "All of us will at one point or another in our life be subjected to adversity. And resilience is very important in influencing vulnerability to psychopathology, particularly mood and anxiety disorders." If resilience is low, it becomes difficult to bounce back from negative experiences. Therefore, adjusting your emotional style—and how you think and react emotionally—is essential for leading the life you aspire to. Davidson adds, "One of my key messages is that the styles are indeed based upon specific brain circuits. And since we know that the brain exhibits plasticity, our styles in fact can be changed through a concept I call neurally inspired behavioural interventions" (Winerman, 2012).

Norman Doidge, a distinguished scientist, doctor, and researcher at the University of Toronto and Columbia University, provides a compelling narrative in his bestselling books, *The Brain That Changes Itself* and *The Brain's Way of Healing*. Doidge states, "Equipped for the first time, with the tools to observe the living brain's microscopic activities, neuroplasticians showed that the brain changes as it works. In 2000, the Nobel Prize for medicine was awarded for demonstrating that, as learning occurs, the connections among nerve cells increase." He further notes that the scientist behind this discovery, Eric Kandel, revealed how learning can 'switch on' genes that alter neural structure. This seminal work laid the foundation for hundreds of studies, confirming that "mental activity is not just a product of the brain but also a shaper of it" (Adams, 2015). Doidge's research highlights remarkable stories of individuals who have overcome significant challenges and achieved personal growth by intentionally rewiring their brains. Through a combination of practical exercises and meditative practices, these individuals have managed to break free from destructive habits, recover from traumatic experiences, and even boost their cognitive functions.

Doidge highlights several transformative cases in his work, showcasing the potential of neuroplasticity. He shares the story of a medical doctor who, after suffering from chronic neck pain due to an injury, trained his brain to "process anything but pain, to weaken his chronic brain circuits." This habit-building process eventually proved curative, permanently stopping his pain. Another compelling example Doidge provides is that of John Pepper, a South African man who used neuroplastic techniques to reverse the symptoms of his Parkinson's disease. Pepper reactivated "existing brain circuits that had fallen into disuse" and retrained them to help him walk again, gradually regaining other motor controls as well. Doidge also covers the curious case of David Webber, a man who successfully cured himself of blindness caused by the autoimmune disease uveitis. Webber's deep meditation and 'reorientation' exercises completely dumbfounded his doctors. These cases powerfully illustrate how directed mental exercises and meditation can lead to significant physical healing and recovery, challenging conventional medical understanding (Doidge, 2016).

Doidge's research operates on the principle that we can actively stimulate 'unused' brain circuits and rewire them to better serve our needs and desires. One technique explored by his team involves using energy source devices, such as low-intensity laser therapies, to manipulate neuron connections in the brain. These laser and light therapies are essentially forms of frequency therapy, given that light energy, like all energy, exists in wavelengths. Notably, his investigations into the use of vibrations have helped an MS patient regain their singing voice, showcasing the practical applications of this approach in restoring lost capabilities. In another case, soundwaves were used to mimic a mother's voice in order to ease or overcome symptoms of autism amongst children on the spectrum (Adams, 2015).

He explains, "All the energies I describe can be easily defined and measured in western terms. The thing is, there are no lights, colours, smells or sounds inside the brain. There are patterns of electrical information and our sense receptors, our retinas, the cochlea in the ear are, in energy terms, transducers. Meaning that what they do is translate one form of energy—sound, light, heat—into another. It is the latter—electrical patterns of energy in the brain—that in one way or another help or cause the brain to sculpt itself, neuroplastically. Somehow or other, thought itself can do that work. It became apparent that this link between mind, brain and energy really is central to who we are and what we do" (Adams, 2015).

Doidge breaks down neuroplastic healing across four categories:

1. **Neurostimulation:** stimulating dormant circuits within the brain to activate them
2. **Neuromodulation:** resetting brain circuits to a neutral state, ensuring they are neither overstimulated nor underactive
3. **Neurorelaxation:** relaxing the brain's circuitry to reduce stress and enhance functionality
4. **Neurodifferentiation and learning:** training the brain to make fine distinctions, enhancing its ability to learn and adapt to new information or situations.

Doidge's framework provides a clear explanation of how modifying the general cellular functions within the brain's neural connections—the electrical circuitry of our minds—can significantly impact overall well-being (Witchalls, 2015).

The science of neuroplasticity reveals that the brain is not static but an adaptable, malleable organ capable of significant change throughout our lives. Doidge highlights that patterns of electricity—or frequency—can be leveraged to modify the brain's structure and function, particularly when it is dormant, stuck, or misfiring. For those looking to adopt a frequency mindset, it's crucial to be active participants in their own neuroplastic journeys. Doidge emphasizes that an individual's willingness and eagerness to engage with a mindful, positive attitude are essential to "making radical brain changes possible" (Gordon, 2015).

Recall the phrase mentioned earlier: "Sow a thought and you reap an action; sow an act and you reap a habit; sow a habit and you reap a character; sow a character and you reap a destiny." I propose that there's a preliminary step *before* sowing a thought itself. While positive thinking and meditation are powerful tools for aligning our minds and bodies with the desired frequencies, we can initiate this alignment even earlier. Instead of relying solely on positive thinking to program our brain activity, we can use frequency to cultivate positive thinking from the outset. Let frequency be the agent that changes your thoughts for you, essentially automating the process! So you see, frequency stimuli can be even more fundamental than thoughts, in the domino effect that will profoundly transform your destiny. Now, let's explore the various kinds of frequencies and how they can be utilized...

UNDERSTANDING BRAINWAVE FREQUENCIES: ALPHA, BETA, THETA, DELTA, GAMMA

The human brain is an electrochemical organ, relying on electrical impulses to control every aspect of your being. Research suggests that an average, fully functioning adult brain can generate up to ten watts of electrical current (Herrmann, 1997). This electrical output manifests as brainwaves.

Brainwaves, or *neural oscillations*, were first identified in 1924 by Hans Berger, who invented the electroencephalogram (EEG). An EEG captures the electrical activity produced by the firing of neurons in the brain. Brainwaves are measured in hertz (Hz), which indicate the number of cycles per second that a frequency occurs.

The brain generates rhythmic patterns of electrical activity that can be categorized into four primary types: alpha, beta, theta, and delta. Each of these brainwave frequencies is associated with specific mental and emotional states, offering us valuable insights into different aspects of our consciousness. To fully embrace the frequency mindset, it's crucial to understand these four categories of brainwaves and their unique functions.

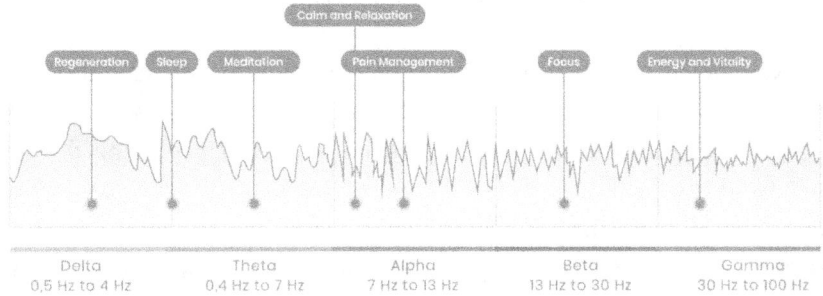

The four primary types of brainwaves range from most to least active. Starting with the most active, we have beta waves. Beta waves are linked to active alertness and are crucial for maintaining focus, analytical thinking, decision-making, and problem-solving. They also play a key role in controlling the body's movements and self-regulation mechanisms. Beta waves oscillate between fifteen to forty cycles per second, typical of a mind that is highly engaged. A person who is alert, concentrating, and thinking clearly is likely experiencing beta waves. The relationship between beta waves and movement is particularly significant in researching motor control disorders, such as Parkinson's disease (Pearce, 2022).

Following beta waves, we have alpha waves, which oscillate between approximately 9 to 14 cycles per second. Alpha waves are associated with a state of relaxed wakefulness and are often linked to enhanced creativity and problem-solving capabilities. Unlike the cognitive arousal characterized by beta waves, alpha waves indicate a more tranquil state of mind. This state is typically observed when a person is resting, reflecting, or engaging in meditation. Research underscores the importance of alpha waves in the creative process. A landmark study in 1978 associated alpha waves with the generation of ideas, particularly during storytelling activities (Martindale, 1978). Another study found that fostering an alpha state could increase the production of original ideas (Lustenberger, 2015). More recently, alpha states have been recognized for their potential in alleviating symptoms of depression and anxiety (Alexander, 2019; Dadashi, 2015). An intriguing aspect of alpha waves is that their resonance—or amplitude—matches the Earth's own resonant frequency. This similarity suggests that this frequency acts as a background energy field influencing our biological circuitry (Dispenza, 2019).

Next in the spectrum are theta brainwaves, which are characterized by greater amplitude and a slower frequency, ranging between five to eight cycles per second. The theta state is conducive to the flow of ideas and is typically activated during repetitive tasks, such as driving on a freeway or taking a jog. In these situations, your mind can wander as part of it operates on autopilot, allowing theta brainwaves to dominate. This state is beneficial as it allows your brain to disengage from active tasks and freely explore other thoughts. Theta brainwaves are often described as facilitating an emotionally 'blissful' experience (Aftanas, 2001) and are linked to heightened intuition and creativity. They are associated with trance-like states where visualization capabilities are enhanced. These brainwaves also play a crucial role in non-deliberate, unintentional awareness or *implicit learning*—this means your brain is absorbing information that you might not consciously recognize at the moment (Loonis, 2017). This makes theta states particularly valuable for creative processes and subconscious problem-solving.

Finally, we come to delta brainwaves, which are the slowest of the four types, ranging between 1.5 and 4 cycles per second. Delta brainwaves are most commonly observed during deep sleep and are crucial for restorative rest. For example, when you climb into bed and read for a while, your brain is likely in a beta state. After you turn off the lights and settle down, your brainwaves shift into alpha, then to theta, and finally transition to delta as you drift into deep sleep. If your delta wave state is interrupted, your body may struggle to rejuvenate properly, affecting your overall health and well-being.

Research has shown that these four brainwave states are universal across humans, regardless of culture or geography. While the brain primarily operates in one state at a time, traces of the other three types are always present to some degree, indicating the complex interplay of neural activities that underpin our mental states (Herrmann, 1997).

In addition to the primary four brainwave types, there is a fifth, less commonly discussed type known as gamma waves. Gamma waves are the highest frequency among the five, surpassing beta waves. However, due to their small amplitude, gamma waves can be challenging to measure, often blending into other types of neural electrochemical activity. A gamma brain state is associated with advanced cognitive functions such as memory and concentration (Pearce, 2022).

Understanding the various brainwaves and the mental states they promote is crucial for adopting a frequency mindset. Brainwaves naturally transition throughout the day, shifting from one type to another, but these shifts don't always align with our current tasks or intentions. That's why gaining control over your brain's electrochemical processes is essential. By training your brain, you can learn to invoke the optimal brainwave state for any given situation. For example, if your mind is in overdrive and you're caught up in excessive thinking, but you need to relax or sleep, your brain is likely stuck in a beta state when it should be transitioning to a delta state. To resolve this, you need to change your frequency.

Traditionally, there have been three main methods used to control and modify brainwave states. Understanding how these methods have been applied until now will help you appreciate the significant advancements made by my Qi Life technologies. Let's briefly explore these traditional approaches to see just how much of a leap forward Qi Life represents.

The three traditional methods of changing your frequency *were...*

1. Neurofeedback
2. Brainwave entrainment
3. Meditation

Neurofeedback therapy is a process that involves monitoring your brainwave activity to identify and recognize the frequencies associated with different feelings and emotions as you experience them. Wearable devices are available to help with this monitoring, and over time, you can learn to identify your brainwave state just by recognizing your emotional state. Dr. Caroline Carney, chief medical officer at Magellan Health, explains, "By seeing how the brain responds to different visual, video, or auditory stimuli, through observing EEG tracings or a visualization of those, it's believed that the brain can be trained on what it needs to do to achieve healthier patterns" (Silva, 2023).

Brainwave entrainment involves using external frequency stimuli to synchronize your brainwave state as desired. Specific frequencies can trigger different states of consciousness or behaviours. As physicist and meditation master C. Maxwell Cade describes it, this method is "a new way of learning, a way of relearning, or realizing for the first time, what the body already knows—how to act, how to feel, even how to heal—if we listen" (Cade, 1979). Neurons in the brain oscillate rhythmically through electrochemical and electromagnetic processes. When external frequencies are introduced, these processes can activate the neocortex—the part of your brain that interacts with the world around you. These oscillation patterns influence your emotional responses, cognitive functions, and motor control (Fries, 2005). A study at Ohio State University demonstrated that "periodic auditory stimulation produces a mixture of evoked and induced, rate-specific and rate-independent increases in brainwave synchronization that are likely to affect various cognitive functions" (Will, 2007). For example, if you're having trouble sleeping, the natural frequencies of your brain during sleep can be mimicked by frequency devices. Exposure to such devices helps your brain realign to encourage healthier sleep patterns. Similarly, this technique can enhance activities like exercise, meditation, studying, creative work, and more. By training your brain's neural processes, you can activate specific emotions and feelings, and even change your genetic functionality through new neural programming, effectively programming your emotions.

Meditation is another effective method for modulating your brainwave state. Different forms of meditation can produce varying effects, but all types are beneficial for influencing desired brainwave states. Research has shown that meditation can significantly increase alpha and theta frequencies, which are associated with relaxation and heightened creativity (Lagopoulos, 2009). Furthermore, studies have found that specific breathing techniques used in many meditation practices can increase alpha waves while decreasing beta waves, which are often linked to active, anxious states. Additionally, meditation and relaxed exercise practices such as yoga are known for their ability to modulate brainwaves. These practices have proven particularly effective in combating stress and anxiety disorders (Kaushik, 2020).

All three methods—neurofeedback, meditation, and brainwave entrainment—can effectively adjust your brain's frequencies. However, neurofeedback equipment can be complex to use, and while meditation is powerful, not everyone has the time to learn advanced techniques or incorporate them into their busy schedules. This is why I advocate for more passive methods like brainwave entrainment. By simply exposing yourself to the right frequencies, you can program the destiny you desire. Yet, like neurofeedback and meditation, traditional brainwave entrainment also needs updating. It's time for a significant overhaul to enhance its benefits and achieve holistic transformation for the mind, body, and spirit. We need to make frequency adjustment quicker and more comprehensive. The goal isn't just to reprogram the brain but to reprogram your *entire body*.

My team has dedicated years to meticulously researching, refining, and testing specific frequencies for particular desires and outcomes. We've observed that many leading figures in neural programming today have not only failed to provide specific solutions for consumers but have also not fully explored the potential of this technology. They've approached it with a narrow mindset, whereas the possibilities should be truly expansive and awe-inspiring. That's why our mission has been to identify which sequences of frequencies are most effective, not just for targeted brainwave entrainment, but also for programming new realities and accessing new levels of consciousness. We achieve this by crafting frequencies designed to reprogram emotions, thought patterns, attitudes, and overall outlook. This comprehensive approach involves radically redefining your energetic field and sets us apart from our competitors. It allows individuals to bypass traditional, lengthy meditation practices and quickly tap into these transformative developments. This opens the door to embracing the frequency mindset in a profound way. Some refer to this broad approach as 'bioresonance'. We call it *Qi Resonance*. Qi Resonance combines ancient wisdom with cutting-edge technology, enabling you to overcome obstacles and shape your destiny like never before. Whether you're looking to completely reinvent yourself or build upon the successes you've already achieved, Qi Resonance offers a way to redefine your personal energy field and infuse proactive abundance into your daily life.

Our technology and devices utilize simple continuous tones, as well as complex sounds called 'higher quantum frequencies' that incorporate as many 5000 tones. These soundwaves are specifically designed to achieve a distinct physical or cognitive outcome. Your brain has the ability to lock onto these soundwaves and synchronize with their resonance, aligning your internal brainwaves with the rhythm of the external sonic stimulus (Thaut, 2015). By programming your thoughts through these frequencies, you're essentially programming your destiny. The beauty of this approach is that it can become habitual and **automatic**, echoing the principles shared by Ralph Waldo Emerson's idea: sow a habit and you reap a destiny. This, I believe, is the secret to long-term, sustainable personal growth and transformation—it needs to become habitual, a part of your nature. Once you integrate this type of resonant automation into your daily routine, you'll wonder how you ever managed without it. Our goal is to make this process streamlined and easily accessible, crafting technology that fits seamlessly into today's busy, complex lifestyles. Our devices are designed not just to encourage the frequency mindset but to make attaining it a tangible reality for anyone, regardless of their daily demands.

Throughout this section, we've explored the practical uses of brainwave frequencies, showing how they can be utilized to improve our daily lives. We've referenced scientific studies, in-depth research, and real-life examples to clearly demonstrate the benefits of understanding and actively engaging with these frequencies.

As we continue to navigate the intricate science of frequency, you'll gain a deeper appreciation for the complex relationship between your thoughts, emotions, and brain activity. The scientific groundwork laid in this chapter underscores the effectiveness of the frequency mindset, equipping you not only with knowledge but also with practical tools to actively sculpt your reality. This foundation ensures that you're well-prepared to apply these insights and techniques to enhance both personal growth and everyday functionality.

CHAPTER 3
REWIRING YOUR BRAIN: THE SCIENCE OF TRANSFORMATION

THE SCIENCE OF PERSONAL TRANSFORMATION

Psychologist Carol Dweck has dedicated her career to exploring human motivation, identifying two primary mindsets through which people navigate life: the growth mindset and the fixed mindset. Her research suggests that adopting a growth mindset is crucial for achieving success. She describes her approach as follows: "My work bridges developmental psychology, social psychology, and personality psychology, and examines the self-conceptions (or mindsets) people use to structure the self and guide their behaviour. My research looks at the origins of these mindsets, their role in motivation and self-regulation, and their impact on achievement and interpersonal processes" (Parrish, 2015). In her book, *Mindset: The New Psychology of Success*, Dweck presents extensive findings supporting her theory. She posits that both our unconscious and conscious thoughts significantly influence our desires and our ability to achieve them (Dweck, 2006). This insight prompts a crucial question: Where do you find yourself on the want-success continuum?

Our exploration of personal transformation begins with an insightful look at the human mind's remarkable capacity for change, highlighted by Dweck's influential research. Her studies show that our beliefs about our abilities significantly influence our life's path, sometimes propelling us toward greater achievements, or conversely, acting as barriers to our success. Those who adopt a growth mindset, believing in their potential for improvement, often enjoy more success and personal growth throughout their lives.

Dweck challenges us with a thought-provoking question: "What are the consequences of thinking that your intelligence or personality is something you can develop, as opposed to something that is a fixed, deep-seated trait?" This question encourages deep self-reflection. The way we perceive ourselves can shape every facet of our lives. The growth mindset, which Dweck promotes, is founded on the belief that your fundamental qualities are things you can develop through effort. It suggests that evolving how you view your abilities can profoundly influence your overall life experience. This mindset fosters a robust curiosity and a continuous desire to learn and grow, rather than a compulsion to constantly prove oneself. She argues, "Why waste time proving over and over how great you are when you could be getting better?" (Dweck, 2006).

Dweck encourages her research subjects to stretch themselves and persist, even when initial attempts don't lead to success. Thriving in the face of challenges and adversity is a fundamental aspect of the growth mindset. This approach involves overcoming deficiencies instead of concealing them, engaging with people who challenge you rather than those who merely flatter you, and seeking experiences that test your beliefs about your abilities rather than sticking to the familiar and safe. Essentially, adopting a growth mindset means learning to be comfortable with being outside of your comfort zone.

Dweck distinguishes between *fixed* and *growth* mindsets according to how each mindset responds to challenges, obstacles, effort, criticism, and the success of others. Each of these metrics reveals how a person with either mindset approaches and navigates their experiences. Let's take a closer look into these distinctions to understand how they shape our reactions and guide our growth.

In a fixed mindset, individuals believe their intelligence and talents are static traits, which leads them to want validation from others, seeking approval to affirm their existing abilities. But this mindset can be quite limiting in the long term. Those with a fixed mindset often avoid challenges, give up easily when faced with obstacles, see effort as futile, dismiss constructive criticism and feedback, and feel threatened by the success of others. Together, these tendencies can cause individuals to plateau early in their lives, ultimately achieving less than their full potential. This mindset is often linked to a *deterministic worldview*, where outcomes are seen as predetermined, and individual actions are believed to have little impact on life's results. If you recognize these traits in yourself, it's important to know that it's possible to break this cycle.

In contrast, someone with a growth mindset sees intelligence as something that can be developed and improved. This mindset fosters a love of learning and an openness to making mistakes, significantly reducing the need for external validation. Over time, this attitude proves to be incredibly beneficial. Those with a growth mindset embrace challenges, persevere in the face of difficulties, see effort as essential for mastering skills, welcome all forms of criticism, and view the successes of others as opportunities to learn and cultivate motivation. These traits collectively promote a personality that is oriented towards continual growth and capable of achieving increasingly higher goals. This perspective is often associated with an *indeterministic worldview*, where the outcomes of our actions are not predetermined but are influenced significantly by our efforts. In this view, what we do profoundly impacts our life's outcomes—*your* actions directly contribute to *your* results.

Perhaps you noticed a common theme across both mindsets, one centred on risk and effort. Those with a growth mindset understand that challenges and obstacles can lead to opportunities and growth. Dweck explains this dynamic well: "As you begin to understand the fixed and growth mindsets, you will see exactly how one thing leads to another—how a belief that your qualities are carved in stone leads to a host of thoughts and actions, and how a belief that your qualities can be cultivated leads to a host of different thoughts and actions, taking you down an entirely different road." To truly embrace a growth mindset—and by extension, a frequency mindset—you must believe that success isn't about being more gifted than others, but about maximizing the gifts you already possess. It's essential to view failure not as a measure of your worth but as a stepping stone for growth and improvement. Moreover, you must recognize that effort and talent are not mutually exclusive; rather, consistent effort can foster and develop talent over time (Parrish, 2015; Dweck, 2006).

To summarize, every challenge, obstacle, and piece of criticism you encounter is an opportunity to step outside your comfort zone and enhance your skills through deliberate practice. It's not that you can't solve the problems you face; it's just that you haven't solved them yet —but you will. By framing problems as 'not yet' situations rather than immediate failures, you open up a pathway to future success instead of trapping yourself in the present. Dweck describes this as the *power of yet* versus the *tyranny of now*. This mindset shift is even observable at the neurological level. Studies have shown that individuals with a fixed mindset react to difficulty, failure, and error with brain activity that tends to be stagnant when faced with adversity. In contrast, those with a growth mindset, who believe their abilities and intelligence can be developed, exhibit dynamic and robust brain activity under the same conditions. Their brains light up with active neuron firing and widespread signalling, reflecting their belief in personal development and resilience (Dweck, 2006).

Much of Dweck's research has focused on how students' learning styles impact their educational outcomes. In one notable study, students were encouraged to push beyond their comfort zones to tackle new and challenging tasks. As a result, not only did the neurons in their brains form new and stronger connections, but their academic performance also improved. Conversely, students who did not adopt this growth mindset experienced a decline in grades, and the anticipated neural connections did not develop. Interestingly, when students initially held to a fixed mindset were later introduced to growth mindset principles and taught accordingly, their grades rebounded (Dweck, 2006).

This ability to recover from setbacks and learn from challenges exemplifies neuroplasticity in action, showing that personal transformation is not only scientifically valid but also heavily dependent on one's *willingness* to embrace and apply these concepts. This underscores the significant impact that mindset has on our capacity to grow and succeed. So, when you next face a challenging situation, consider how you will approach it cognitively. A pivotal question might be: what facilitates the shift from a fixed to a growth mindset?

NEUROPLASTICITY: THE BRAIN'S ADAPTIVE POWER

Answering how we can shift from a fixed to a growth mindset is intricately linked to the concept of neuroplasticity—the brain's extraordinary ability to adapt and reorganize itself through experience and practice. Neuroscientist Michael Merzenich's pioneering research is a cornerstone in this field, demonstrating how targeted training can significantly alter the brain's structure and functionality.

Historically, the consensus in neuroscience was that neuroplasticity was predominantly an early childhood phenomenon, tied to the dynamic and rapidly developing brains of young children. However, recent advancements in the field have debunked this notion. We now understand that neuroplasticity, or the brain's ability to 'remodel' itself, can occur at any age, and is possible even in brains that have experienced damage. The primary difference with age is how the brain regulates its own plasticity. In children, plasticity is almost boundless and constantly active, but as we age, our brain's plasticity tends to be more dependent on behavioural context and outcomes (Swain, 1993; Merzenich, 1996, 2001, 2013; Weinberger, 2004; Gilbert, 2009). This means that while the conditions for plasticity are perpetually 'on' during childhood, adults may require more deliberate external stimuli to engage those same neural mechanisms effectively.

The optimal way to activate neuroplasticity involves the production of neuromodulatory neurotransmitters, which facilitate enduring changes in the brain's electrochemical connections. Recent research, including studies by Merzenich, has clarified the 'rules' governing the release and effects of neuromodulators on learning and memory across the lifespan (Nakamura and Sakaguchi, 1990; Sara and Segal, 1991; Steiner, 2006; Smith, 2011). Merzenich and his team have demonstrated that the strength, selectivity, and reliability of these neuromodulators can be significantly enhanced through intensive training in most individuals (Merzenich, 2014).

This research underscores that neurological inputs can effectively modify neurobehaviour, suggesting that plasticity can be cultivated and enhanced in various neurological functions such as perception, memory, attention, and suppression of distractions. The critical element in neuroplasticity is the strength of the connections, or synapses, within our brain circuits. Essentially, the intensity of the frequency input directly influences the strength of the neurological output. As Donald Hebb, a Canadian psychologist, famously stated, "What fires together, wires together" (Hebb, 1949). When we learn a new skill or ability, our brain circuitry adapts through the continued experience and practice of that skill, leading to specialization. This turns our brain into a "master receiver and master controller" of all inputs and actions supporting that mastery (Merzenich, 2014).

The process of neuroplasticity is remarkable due to the collaborative interaction among the brain's neurons. When one set of neurons fires, it not only activates but also forms synapses with neighbouring neurons, engaging more of the brain in the process. This simultaneous, cooperative activity enhances the brain's power and reliability in responding to inputs. Neuroplasticity can be viewed as neural teamwork, playing a crucial role in your brain's ability to process information effectively (Edelman, 1987; Merzenich and Jenkins, 1993; Merzenich and de Charms, 1996; Merzenich, 2013).

Researchers like Merzenich have greatly advanced our understanding of the complex dynamics of brain change and the physiological rules governing plasticity. Their findings have paved the way for optimizing conditions that foster positive neural adjustments, processing, and behavioral functions. With these insights, "we can more directly target neurological improvement" and aid in the restoration or recovery of brain functions, particularly in cases of pre-existing damage or impairment (Merzenich, 2014). The benefits of neuroplastic therapies are twofold: they not only promote cognitive improvement in healthy individuals but also offer significant rehabilitative potential for those with damaged brain structures due to illness or injury. The possibilities of neuroplastic therapies are virtually limitless, positioning neuroplasticity as a scientific means to *game your brain* for success. (Medeiros, 2017). Just as we've discovered 'life hacks' for various aspects of our daily lives, neuroplasticity represents the ultimate life hack.

Gaming or hacking your brain can unlock new abilities and lead to a more practical approach to life. Research indicates that cognitive decline begins in your 20s and 30s. From this point, the brain's speed and reliability start to wane—peripheral vision narrows, hearing becomes less sharp, and both memory and attention span deteriorate. Moreover, as we age, we often gravitate toward a more fixed mindset: becoming less social, more egocentric, and our confidence and willingness to take risks declines (Medeiros, 2017). This is a natural challenge we face due to biological aging.

So, how do we combat this decline? The answer lies in neuroplastic therapy. To leverage your brain's neuroplastic capabilities and foster a strong frequency and growth mindset, it is crucial to continuously challenge your brain. Neuroscientist Adam Gazzaley emphasizes, "Like every organ in our bodies, the brain undergoes changes in how it performs. You see it in your muscles, your bones, your hair—and you feel it in your brain. That is not helped by people seeking comfort and a less demanding life when they are older. The fact is that the brain is still plastic even when they are 70 or 80 years old. It can still be optimized—but instead, many people unwittingly accelerate its deterioration." This insight underscores the importance of actively engaging the brain throughout life to slow cognitive aging and enhance brain function.

Just as you lift weights to strengthen your muscles, your brain also needs exercise to stay strong, and neuroplastic therapies can be thought of as a gym for your mind. We have the capability—and the responsibility—to continuously enhance and expand our cognitive abilities. Personal transformation requires active engagement rather than remaining on autopilot, repeatedly doing the same things and thinking the same thoughts. Albert Einstein famously captured this notion when he said, "Insanity is doing the same thing over and over again and expecting different results." Neuroplasticity presents us with a promising outlook for a productive and enriched future, one that is built on diverse experiences and fresh possibilities. However, embracing this opportunity requires a conscious decision from each of us. We must actively *choose* to adopt and nurture a growth and frequency mindset, stepping out of our comfort zones and challenging our brains to ensure continuous development and improvement.

HOW BRAINWAVE FREQUENCIES AND MINDSET SHAPE YOUR HEALTH

As we explore brainwave frequencies further, we uncover their pivotal role in facilitating changes in mindset, which importantly extends beyond cognitive and perceptual health. There's compelling evidence that shifts in frequency can also directly affect physical health. Neuroscientist Richard Davidson's research on meditation provides a powerful example of this connection. His studies reveal that modifying brainwave patterns through meditation can lead to significant improvements in the immune system.

Davidson and his team conducted an experiment where they measured electrical brain activity in subjects before and after receiving an influenza vaccine. One group of participants engaged in regular mindfulness and meditation sessions, while the other group did not. The results were quite remarkable. The group that meditated showed an increase in neural activity that correlated with a heightened antibody response to the influenza virus. This research demonstrates "that a short program in mindfulness meditation produces demonstrable effects on brain and immune function. These findings suggest that meditation may change brain and immune function in positive ways..." (Davidson, 2003).

Davidson's work has linked meditative mindfulness to mental and physical health improvements, particularly in managing chronic pain. His research suggests that meditation enhances awareness of the present, hones focused attention skills, and cultivates positive emotions, which collectively contribute to pain management (University of Wisconsin-Madison, 2003).

David Black of the University of Southern California has conducted similar research, exploring the relationship between mindfulness meditation and the immune system, examining five immune system parameters: circulating and stimulated inflammatory proteins, cellular transcription factors and gene expression, immune cell count, immune cell aging, and antibody response. His findings indicate that meditation has a beneficial impact on cell-mediated immunity, inflammation, and biological aging (Black, 2016).

Further supporting these findings, another study observed significant changes in gene expression related to stress response, immune function, and metabolism in subjects who practiced meditation. This research highlighted enhancements in cellular health, specifically noting improvements in acute-phase wound healing and inflammation. The study also found that meditation positively influenced protein production related to dementia and depression risk and promoted healthy aging by boosting the activity of telomere maintenance genes and enzymes (Espel, 2016).

Consider the journey of someone grappling with anxiety, stress, or a weakened immune system. Through a committed meditation practice, this individual can not only transform their emotional state but also significantly improve their physical health. The studies mentioned above provide strong evidence of how such transformations are not just possible but documented. Traditionally, discussions in medicine and science tend to compartmentalize the brain and the body; however, the brain is unequivocally a part of the body. It logically follows—and is robustly supported by research—that a healthy mind fosters a healthy brain, which in turn contributes to a healthy body. When these elements are in sync, the spirit thrives as well. This holistic perspective embodies what is achieved through a growth and frequency mindset. It's about aligning all of our systems, tuning them through the power of frequency so that they resonate harmoniously. Improving your frequency means improving your life!

PRACTICAL TECHNIQUES FOR BRAIN REWIRING

To provide you with practical tools for brain rewiring, let's look into the techniques substantiated by neuroscience research, particularly the work of Sara Lazar on mindfulness meditation. Lazar's research has demonstrated that regular mindfulness meditation not only promotes a sense of peace and physical relaxation but also induces structural changes in the brain. These changes enhance memory, reduce stress, and aid in the modulation of emotional processing (Lazar, 2005).

Lazar explains the significance of these findings: "Although the practice of meditation is associated with a sense of peacefulness and physical relaxation, practitioners have long claimed that meditation also provides cognitive and psychological benefits that persist throughout the day. This study demonstrates that changes in brain structure may underlie some of these reported improvements and that people are not just feeling better because they are spending time relaxing."

Lazar's studies have documented a literal thickening of the cerebral cortex in areas related to emotional integration and attention, such as the hippocampus, where increases in grey matter density were observed. This structural change not only enhances emotion, memory, and attention but also positively affects self-awareness, introspection, and compassion. Additionally, Lazar's research noted decreases in grey matter in the amygdala, which is heavily involved in processing anxiety and stress (McGreevey, 2011). This evidence underscores that meditation not only rewires but also physically remodels the brain, illustrating the profound impact of frequency changes in the brain's electrochemical processes.

Britta Hölzel, a colleague of Lazar, reflects on these findings, stating, "It is fascinating to see the brain's plasticity and that, by practicing meditation, we can play an active role in changing the brain and can increase our well-being and quality of life." Amishi Jha, a neuroscientist at the University of Miami, suggests that these findings could also have implications for treating complex emotional conditions such as post-traumatic stress disorder (PTSD).

Imagine someone caught in the whirlwind of a hectic and stressful life, who begins to practice mindfulness meditation daily and experiences significant enhancements in overall well-being. Or consider someone suffering from PTSD or other trauma-related issues, who finds relief through the frequency-modulating effects of meditation. These scenarios illustrate the transformative power of frequency adjustment in achieving a meditative or relaxed state of mind. This is where technologies like those developed at Qi Life come into play. By facilitating a meditative or relaxed state, such technologies make individuals more receptive to positive frequency adjustments. Our Qi Coil™, for example, is designed to optimize this process.

One of the unique aspects of these compact copper coils is their ability to maximize energy cultivation and dramatically enhance holistic wellness by shielding you from the pervasive electromagnetic pollution encountered daily. By protecting you from these negative energy sources and simultaneously exposing you to targeted positive frequencies, the Qi Coil™ makes it easier to rewire and remodel your brain. Our users have reported a range of electromagnetically induced benefits:

- Improved mood
- Accelerated regeneration
- Boosted energy and stamina
- Enhanced mental clarity and focus
- Improved pain management
- Heightened sexual wellness and performance
- Reduced stress and anxiety
- Sounder sleep
- Elevated meditation
- Increased relaxation response

- Strengthened biofield

Our technology creates a powerful electromagnetic field that can cover an entire room, offering a contactless and non-invasive way to enhance your well-being. Our accompanying webApp (members.Qi-Coil.com) and our Resonant Console Tablet provide access to thousands of frequencies, allowing you to customize your experience to target specific symptoms and promote desired physical and mental outcomes. Each frequency serves as a precise instruction, delivered at the cellular level using electromagnetism. This not only helps clear surrounding electromagnetic pollution but also helps you draw in positive energy, attract abundance, and improve your ability to manifest your goals.

In this chapter, I've shared the scientific foundation supporting the brain's capacity for rewiring, which influenced the development of our Qi Life devices, but we've also conducted our own qualitative research. For example, in developing the Qi Coil™, we utilized advanced GDV (gas discharge visualization) cameras to measure the energy emissions around users' bodies. Results showed that after just thirty minutes of using the Qi Coil™, users' bio-energy levels increased by 27%. We also observed that gaps in their biofields, which could leave them vulnerable to harmful external energies, were significantly reduced.

These GDV readings further highlighted enhancements in the energy levels of the immune and nervous systems, affecting vital areas such as the thyroid, liver, spine, and coronary vessels. The before-and-after comparisons in our studies not only demonstrate that electromagnetic pollution can be effectively counteracted, but they also illustrate that the resonant harmony of energy within and surrounding the human body can be restored and synchronized.

Our internal product surveys have documented extraordinary results from our users and the effects that our devices and technology have had across many metrics.

- 96% experienced a reduction in pain
- 89% experienced an increase in strength and stamina
- 85% experienced enhanced mental clarity and energy levels

And the difference between our users' experiences versus the everyday non-user is remarkable, as seen in the chart below…

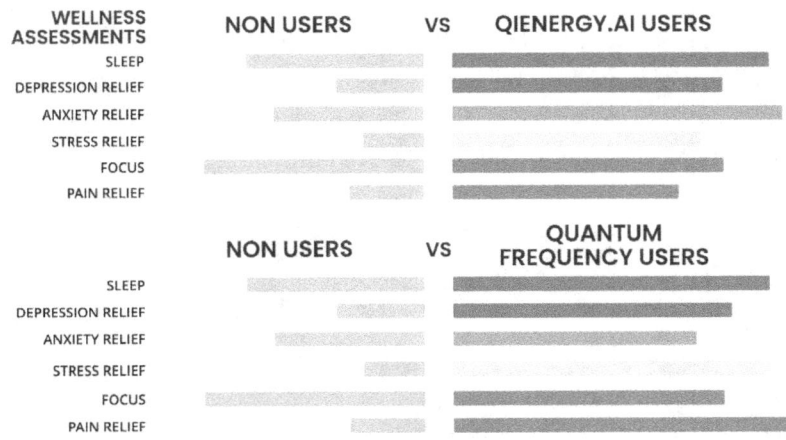

Thousands of people have tried our Qi Coil™ with dramatic results that have completely changed their lives. I'm reminded of so many of their transformative stories… Take Melany, for instance, who faced her darkest fears when doctors diagnosed her with a potentially cancerous breast lump. She lived under the shadow of anxiety, not knowing what the future held. Providence brought her to Qi Coil™, using it for 45 days. To her relief and surprise, not only did the lump vanish by her next medical exam, but her chronic anemia also improved as a bonus, giving her a new lease on life.

Then there's John, whose chronic shoulder pain made each day a struggle. The pain had confined him, making simple tasks like lifting his arm excruciating. With little left to lose, he tried a Qi Coil™ session. Miraculously, the pain that had been his constant companion melted away almost instantly, allowing him freedom of movement he hadn't felt in years.

Similarly, Susan's father was grappling with debilitating Alzheimer's symptoms, which clouded his memory and disoriented him in his own home. After just one Qi Coil™ session, she noticed significant improvements in his cognitive functions, regaining a level of independence and mental clarity that both they and their family thought were lost.

Jeff's story is equally compelling. Suffering from severe back pain due to an old sports injury, he had almost given up hope of living without pain. Skeptical but desperate, he decided to give Qi Coil™ a try. Within minutes of his first session, a soothing warmth spread across his back, easing the pain. By the next morning, the relentless pain that had overshadowed his life was completely gone.

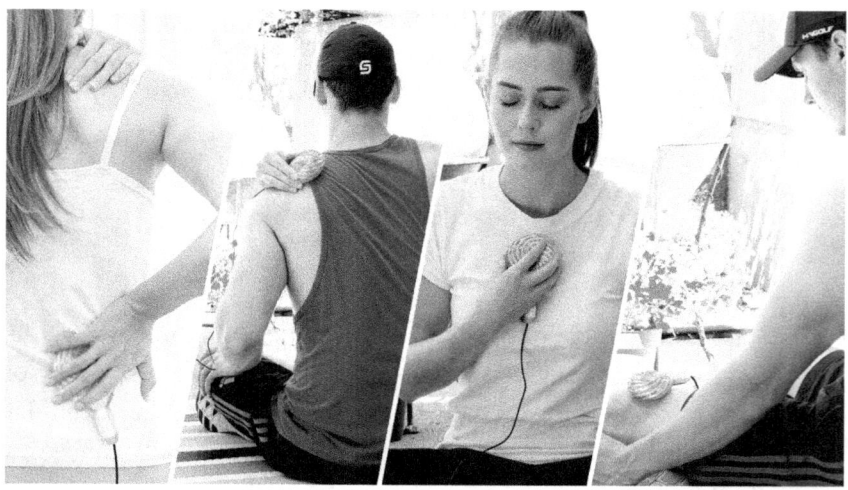

Finally, take George, who suffered from severe neck pain that restricted his movement and impacted his sleep. After trying various therapies with no success, he turned to Qi Coil™. After a few sessions, his pain had subsided, allowing him to return to his daily activities and enjoy a full night's sleep. Stories like these are testament to the revolutionary power of embracing new healing technologies, offering not just relief but a new path forward in life.

As we further navigate the science of transformation, remember that each scientific discovery is more than just a collection of data; it represents a gateway to personal growth and change. By integrating scientific findings with relatable stories, I aim to equip you with both the practical tools and the motivation needed to tap into the incredible potential of your own mind. But as we speak on mindfulness and meditation, it's important to emphasize that it's an *active* process, not a passive one. They are not means of escaping reality but ways to engage with it more fully. As Zen master Thich Nhat Hanh eloquently put it, "Meditation is not evasion; it is a serene encounter with reality."

When we align our mind, body, and spirit with the right frequencies, we're not just passively existing; we're actively shaping the reality we choose and manifest for ourselves. This active engagement is why we refer to the underlying principles of these findings as the *science of transformation*. Mindfulness and the recalibration of your energy are not merely performative or methods of escape—they are transformative processes. By rewiring and remodelling your brain, you open the door to fundamentally rebuilding your life.

CHAPTER 4
TRANSFORMING THOUGHTS INTO REALITY

UNLOCKING THE PINEAL GLAND: WHERE SCIENCE MEETS SPIRITUALITY

Visualization is the foundation of all manifestation efforts. To achieve your goals, you must first clearly envision them. There's a part of your body that plays a crucial role in this process—and I'm not talking about your eyes, at least not the ones you might think. I'm referring to your *third eye*, also known as your pineal gland.

The pineal gland is a small, pine cone-shaped endocrine gland located deep within your brain. Its primary biological function is the production of melatonin, which helps regulate your sleep patterns and influences your central nervous system. However, the significance of the pineal gland goes far beyond this basic function. Extensive historical and cultural perspectives suggest it plays a critical role in our broader spiritual and metaphysical capacities.

Traveling back to ancient Greece, we encounter some of the earliest recorded mentions of the pineal gland by Herophilus, known as history's first anatomist, and later by the physician Galen. They regarded the pineal gland as a critical mediator for the flow of the body's 'vital spirits' or *pneuma*—a concept similar to what other cultures have termed *life force* or *qi energy* (Choudhry, 2011). Centuries later, in the 17th century, the renowned scientist and philosopher René Descartes elevated the pineal gland's significance, calling it "the principal seat of the soul and the place in which all our thoughts are formed." He believed that the soul was connected to the body through the pineal gland, thus playing a crucial role in mediating bodily and spiritual functions (Lockhorst, 2015; Descartes, 2002). In 1918, Swedish scientist Nils Holmgren furthered our understanding by identifying that the pineal gland contained cells similar to those in the retina, confirming its photosensitivity (Wurtman, 1965). This discovery revealed that the pineal gland is highly responsive to light, which is a form of energy or frequency. This supported older cultural assertions, like those of ancient India, which referred to the pineal gland as a '*third eye*', adding a modern scientific validation to a long-held belief.

Cultures with millennia of meditative traditions have long revered the third eye as a profound source of knowledge—a sort of sixth sense. The Chinese, the Tibetans, the Indians, the Egyptians and so many more all spoke of this concept, even if they didn't necessarily connect it to the physical structure of the pineal gland that more modern science has revealed. They recognized its significance and believed that this critical part of the body could tap into higher energy fields, serving as a gateway to divine or universal connections. The consistent reverence for the third eye across diverse cultures highlights its importance, mirroring the wisdom imparted by these ancient societies. They under-stood that this vital element could be harnessed to access expansive, higher states of consciousness. But recognizing the presence of the third eye leads to an even greater inquiry: how do you unlock its potential? Ancient wisdom provides insights into this as well. Let's explore these past contexts a little further…

THE PINEAL GLAND IN SPIRITUAL PRACTICES – THE THIRD EYE

Hindu culture teaches that the third eye, also known as the ajna chakra, is a critical gateway to higher knowledge and serves as a shield against negativity and evil influences. The term 'ajna' means to perceive and command, reflecting the Hindu view of the third eye as a confluence of intuition and intellect, enabling profound insight and control over one's spiritual and intellectual faculties (Dhillon, 2009; Vishnudevananda, 1988). Activation of the third eye in Hindu tradition is believed to facilitate communication with the world and even access information from the past and future.

In Buddhist culture, the third eye is seen as the central point of consciousness, essential for achieving enlightenment that transcends the capabilities of the other senses.

Taoist philosophy offers similar understandings to its Hindu and Buddhist counterparts, but emphasizes the manipulation of energy in more nuanced ways. Taoism particularly advocates for the practice of qigong to train the third eye, aiming to tune the mind with universal vibrations. Proper alignment through this practice is thought to unlock more advanced states of meditation and enlightenment. This perspective considers the third eye as a primary energy centre of the body (Jefferson, 1982).

In philosophical discourse, the concept of the third eye is often synonymous with the 'mind's eye', a term dating back to ancient Roman philosopher Cicero, who referred to it as the *mentis oculi*. This concept describes the mind's ability to visualize images without the aid of physical sight, essentially the brain's capacity to imagine. Cicero's view suggests that our mental imagery allows us to 'see' things internally, leveraging our imagination. For example, if you are asked to imagine an apple, most people can conjure an image of an apple in their minds—some in vivid detail, others in more basic forms. Modern science, however, still grapples with understanding how this process works. As John Ratey, a professor of psychiatry, points out, "As humans, we have the ability to see with the mind's eye—to have a perceptual experience in the absence of visual input" (Ratey, 2001). This ability varies significantly among individuals. Some people visualize in two dimensions, others in three, and while some can envision detailed textures like the skin of an apple, others may only see basic shapes and colours. Biologists and physiologists have yet to fully explain this capability. It's possible that the explanation does not lie solely within the physical brain but extends beyond it—perhaps to more universal or cosmic energy forces. This perspective suggests that activating our third eye could be akin to enhancing our mind's eye, potentially unlocking a more advanced state of consciousness.

The ancient Egyptians valued the pineal gland, or third eye, seeing it as the centre of the soul. They linked it to the 'Eye of Horus' symbol, which stood for healing, well-being, and protection. Interestingly, if you place this symbol over the part of the brain where the pineal gland is located, you will see that the symbol perfectly matches the inner structures of the brain surrounding the gland. Modern scientists have determined that this isn't a coincidence. Even though the Egyptians didn't have modern technology to study the brain's structure, they were advanced in medicine and anatomy for their time. The Eye of Horus symbol shows that the Egyptians had a deep understanding of the human nervous system (ReFaey, 2019).

Examining these ancient cultures and their timeless wisdom informs us that they each understood this unique and peculiar part of the brain as something truly important to the human experience. They believed it was a gateway to higher consciousness, enlightenment, and deeper personal connections. It is this *gateway* that we'll explore next.

YOUR PINEAL GLAND: GATEWAY TO HIGHER CONSCIOUSNESS

Unlocking the potential of the pineal gland as a gateway to higher awareness has long been ingrained in shamanic practices. Accessing realms of greater wisdom and perception is considered the pinnacle of human experience. A crucial part of this journey involves recognizing that the information our five senses provide is not the complete picture. There is a reality around us that we are not fully connected to on a regular basis. Opening and activating the third eye allows us to see truths that were previously hidden. "Just as the owl is blind to the light of the day, we are blind to the spiritual world and are unable to see phenomena that really do exist" (Jamal, 2002).

In Islamic Sufism, mystics discuss their own version of the third eye, referred to as the 'inner eye' or 'eye of the heart'. In order to open it, they contend that you have to be connected and alert to the events of your life. By doing so, you may see things that are not apparent otherwise. Sufis believe that our typical state of awareness makes it difficult to perceive things that are right before us, much like a fish doesn't see the ocean it swims through or how we fail to see the air we breathe. They teach that *spiritual* or universal energy is omnipresent, but invisible to most because we are too busy questioning its where-abouts rather than realizing it is all around us, visible in everything. "If we could take the soul out of the body, we would realize that we always had the spirit" (Jamal, 2002).

Sufi teachings emphasize that to perceive the unseen, one must look with the heart rather than with the eyes. The 'inner eye' is thus situated within the heart, which, when open to the universe or God, allows one to see the invisible, hence the term 'eye of the heart'. This kind of vision is described as *seeing through certainty*. Imam Ali stated, "The eyes cannot see God clearly, but the heart will come to" (Jafari, 2020).

This belief is echoed in various indigenous cultures around the world. For example, tribes in North-West Australia hold that spirits grant those who are willing to submit the ability to open an inner eye. This enables their shamans to see the invisible, track offenders, and foresee dangers and obstacles (Coate, 1966).

Shamanic rituals have historically played a crucial role in exploring the third eye or pineal gland, particularly through the use of plants and herbs. Substances like frankincense have been used for millennia to stimulate the third eye and encourage spiritual experiences. Similar properties are attributed to mugwort, blue lotus flower, coriander, ayahuasca, and others. Shamans have traditionally used special brews, teas, baths, and incense as tools to access other realms, achieve new levels of consciousness, and connect with unseen energy forces. These practices help to amplify energy, calm the mind for clearer reception of external inputs, and enable connections to dream realms.

These examples illustrate diverse cultural and spiritual efforts to access higher awareness—of oneself, one's environment, and beyond. This pursuit of the *beyond* is a theme that recurs across numerous civilizations throughout history. It prompts us to ask what these societies were seeking, and what did they manage to discover, achieve, and manifest once they crossed that threshold? The use of plant-based and herbal aids in shamanic ritual practices is particularly fascinating and worthy of deeper exploration. These methods are not only steeped in ancient tradition but are also increasingly supported by modern science, often in surprising ways.

SCIENTIFIC INSIGHTS INTO PINEAL GLAND ACTIVATION

From a scientific standpoint, one of the most intriguing roles of the pineal gland is its production of DMT (dimethyltryptamine), often called the 'spirit molecule' due to its psychoactive and psychedelic properties when ingested. Intriguingly, the pineal gland naturally produces DMT in the process of synthesizing serotonin and melatonin. Chemically, lab-synthesized DMT is very similar to psilocin or LSD. "Substances like LSD, psilocin, and DMT, under the appropriate circumstances, can all produce classical hallucinogenic experiences that are qualitatively indistinguishable from one another" (Miller, 2014).

The natural occurrence of DMT in the pineal gland and its profound psychotropic effects have fascinated clinical researcher Rick Strassman. Strassman, a long-time Zen Buddhist practitioner, observed early on in his research that there were striking similarities between the out-of-body experiences induced by advanced meditation and those triggered by psychedelic substances. This observation led him to propose that the pineal gland's function might be fundamentally linked to the concept of the third eye, suggesting a biological basis for spiritual and metaphysical experiences. Strassman's insights prompted further exploration into whether the pineal gland could be converting melatonin or serotonin into DMT, thus acting as a portal to spiritual or non-physical realities. "This tiny organ, the 'seat of the soul' or 'third eye' of the ancients, might produce DMT or similar substances by simple chemical alterations... Perhaps it is DMT, released by the pineal, that opens the mind's eye to spiritual, or non-physical, realities" Grob (2002). This hypothesis has laid the groundwork for extensive research by Strassman and others.

In his book *Am I Dreaming?*, James Kingsland discusses how both meditation and psychedelics can reduce connectivity and activity in the brain's default synaptic network. This essentially disrupts the standard flow of electromagnetic energy in the brain and opens up new neural pathways. Kingsland notes that substances like DMT "appear to 'reboot' the brain, providing an opportunity to unlearn maladaptive programming [...] and replace it with healthier patterns of thought and behavior" (Kingsland, 2019).

These profound experiences with substances like DMT are about more than just altering perception; they break down mental and spiritual barriers, allowing individuals to perceive alternate realities. This process can be likened to a vision quest that dramatically expands self-awareness, helping people to see themselves, others, and their surroundings in a completely new light. Imagine the brain as a radio antenna: it's already tuned to the universe's frequencies, but certain states can amplify these frequencies, potentially offering new insights and perspectives. What would a glimpse into these alternate realities provide you with? A different sense of self? A reimagined sense of what's possible?

Both Strassman and Kingsland have explored these topics extensively over the past few decades, though the interest in altered states of consciousness extends back much further. The fascination with the intersections of mystic shamanism, advanced meditation, and psychedelic experiences was particularly pronounced in the scientific community during the 1950s and 1960s. During that era, researchers and even governments investigated how these states could be harnessed for various purposes, including military applications. Initially, the focus wasn't on DMT but on substances like psilocybin. Notable studies, such as the 'Good Friday Experiment' at Harvard or the Johns Hopkins trials, involved dosing subjects with psychedelics to observe the effects. One striking outcome from these experiments was the profound impact on the participants; nearly all described their experiences as life-changing, ranking them among the most significant events of their lives (Beres, 2020). Many of Strassman's subjects similarly reported their experiences as enlightening journeys, or in colloquial terms, a 'trip'.

Many who have experienced psychedelic episodes report a sensation of 'traveling' during their experiences, a phenomenon that Strassman closely associates with the pineal gland. Intriguingly, he notes that the pineal gland first becomes visible in fetal development scans around the 49-day mark. This duration matches precisely with what Buddhist scriptures describe as the length of a soul's 'in-between state,' as detailed in the *Tibetan Book of the Dead*. This text describes the soul's journey post-death, lingering for a period before moving on. Strassman speculates, "Perhaps the life-force of a human enters the fetus at forty-nine days through the pineal, and it may leave the body, at death, through the pineal. This coming and going would be marked by the release of DMT by the pineal, mediating awareness of these awesome events" (Strassman, 2000).

Another dimension of these 'travels' includes a feeling of shedding the self, or more specifically, the ego. Research indicates that during a psychedelic trip, the parts of the brain tied to ego or self-recognition are temporarily suppressed, enabling an individual to feel unified with their surroundings rather than distinct from them. Strassman refers to this as a "sense of oneness." Participants in his studies often describe it as feeling at one with the universe. It appears that DMT and similar substances facilitate new pathways for energy flow within the brain that transcend individual consciousness and align with a more universal consciousness. This opens up individuals to ideas, visions, and possibilities previously unconsidered in their normal state of mind.

Pharmacologist Richard Miller highlights that those drawn to psychedelic experiences or aiming to activate their third eye are often "looking for deeply profound spiritual experiences and a sense of connection, a sense of energy, a sense of being in touch with their own unconscious and their own deeper levels of the mind" (Miller, 2017).

This drive to explore beyond the everyday reality, to experience an *alternate side*, is not a modern phenomenon. The pursuit of opening the third eye spans millennia, and the use of natural psychedelic substances like DMT as a means to facilitate this experience is a deeply rooted tradition. For instance, the Tucano tribes of modern-day Colombia and Brazil use ayahuasca and other brews during their Yurupari ceremonies to mark the transition from boyhood to manhood. These rituals serve to facilitate a passage from one life phase to another, echoing the soul's phase shifts described in *The Tibetan Book of the Dead* (Beres, 2020).

Research by scientists like Strassman has significantly linked the pineal gland to the effects of substances like DMT, shedding light on ancient wisdom through the lens of modern science. We're now beginning to understand not only the consciousness-expanding capabilities of the pineal gland—the third eye—but also recognizing that substances like DMT, which are naturally produced in the body, could have even broader applications than previously understood. This ongoing exploration is revealing new possibilities for how these substances might be used to deepen our awareness and enhance our connection to universal frequencies.

We're also seeing new research that shows that such substances can play a critical role in addressing ailments like addiction and depression. Ethnobotanist Jonathan Ott has suggested that while higher consciousness or out-of-body experiences can "reveal to us the sublime grandeur of our universe," the smaller-scale medicinal benefits derived from these experiences, facilitated by synthetic versions of these substances, could be key to addressing numerous modern health issues—both mental and physical (Schultes, 2001).

This is why DMT is often referred to as the *spirit molecule*. Its intrinsic link with the pineal gland acts as a kind of *scientific third eye*, opening the minds of researchers to new ways of thinking and acknowledging that the key to understanding ourselves might be hidden deep within our brains. The pineal gland, a component recognized by ancient civilizations for millennia, is only now being fully appreciated by the scientific community. We are beginning to grasp the importance of activating the pineal gland, which could provide profound insights into our consciousness and health. As we continue to gain clearer focus in scientific inquiries, we set the stage for the next part of this discussion—exploring how clarity and focus themselves are pivotal to fully unlocking the potential of the pineal gland.

SECRETS OF THE THIRD EYE: A PRACTICAL GUIDE TO PINEAL GLAND ACTIVATION

Did you know there's a part of your brain that acts like a filter, managing the flow of information between your brain and body? This *filter*, known as the Reticular Activating System (RAS), is located at the top of the spinal column and stretches a few inches upward. It plays a crucial role in filtering information, directing your attention, and shaping your perception of reality. The RAS also acts as a gatekeeper between being awake and unconscious, helping to regulate your sleep cycles. It's considered one of the most important parts of your brain with regard to your consciousness (Jang, 2020; Edlow, 2012).

On a more technical level, the RAS processes about eight million bits of information per second, while your entire brain processes around eleven million bits per second. This means the RAS handles most of the work in filtering your sensory inputs, which your brain then turns into thoughts, feelings, and emotions. The role of the RAS is vital for maintaining cognitive clarity and helping you function effectively in your daily life.

One of the biggest hurdles people often face when trying to manifest their desires is the difficulty in maintaining sharp focus and clear visualization of their goals. To properly manifest, you have to be decisive, focussed, and your attention has to be concentrated with a level of consistency and repetitiveness. This is why the RAS is so crucial. The RAS acts as a sensory filter—if it's not aligned with your true objectives, it can flood you with distracting thoughts, emotions, and feelings. These distractions can hinder your ability to overcome obstacles, see clearly, and even prevent you from opening your third eye. As neuroscientist and philosopher Amit Ray points out, the RAS "can be either your friend or your foe as a coach. With its help, you are awake, alert, and engaged. If it works against you, you will be sluggish, sleepy and dull, and your visualization may backfire" (Ray, 2021).

The RAS plays a crucial role in determining which information is prioritized and filtered through to your brain, largely based on your mindset, habits, and repeated exposure to certain stimuli. This 'programming' of the RAS is influenced by various external inputs, including past experiences and the people around you. For instance, if you are considering buying a new car and have a specific model or colour in mind, you might start noticing that car model more frequently. This phenomenon occurs because your RAS is filtering information relevant to your interests, making that car model appear more prevalent. However, this function of the RAS can extend beyond neutral observations. If someone frequently belittles you, or if you perceive that a coworker dislikes you, your RAS might prioritize negative feedback, reinforcing those unpleasant feelings. This is known as confirmation bias, where your subconscious seeks to confirm its existing beliefs, whether they are positive, like high self-esteem, or negative, such as self-doubt or fear. This bias can lead to a cycle where your RAS continues to emphasize information that aligns with your current beliefs, which can be counterproductive if you are trying to change or grow. In essence, while the RAS aims to protect your brain by filtering in what it deems most relevant, it can sometimes hinder personal development by focusing too much on confirming pre-existing notions.

Visualization is crucial because it helps reprogram your RAS to filter information in a way that aligns with your intentions. The ultimate aim is to condition your RAS to emphasize positive inputs over negative ones. While it's impossible—and not desirable—to eliminate all negative inputs (some are essential for recognizing dangers), enhancing the flow of positive information can significantly boost your overall mindset and your ability to activate your pineal gland and open your third eye.

How can you promote more positive filtration by your RAS? It begins with clear visualization. Start by defining your goal and vividly imagining every aspect of achieving it. Clear visualization boosts motivation, which in turn sharpens your focus, making the steps toward your goal clearer. This clarity breeds what some call 'possibility thinking'—the knack for seeing positive outcomes in every situation. As you adopt this mindset, you'll start noticing more resources and opportunities that can aid in achieving your goals, allowing you to reach them faster and more effectively.

When you engage in visualization, you're not just imagining success; you're actively aligning your RAS with your goals. This alignment makes you more attuned to perceiving and prioritizing information, relationships, and resources pertinent to your objectives—details that might previously have been filtered *OUT*. This enhanced perception reinforces your brain's ability to identify and focus on goal-relevant information, effectively doubling down on the process and further strengthening your RAS. Visualization also restructures your brain's wiring. Think of it like walking through a field repeatedly; over time, a clear path forms. Similarly, frequent positive visualization strengthens neural connections and forges new neural pathways, enhancing the efficiency and flow of mental energy. This not only reprograms your RAS but also rewires your entire brain, establishing robust neural pathways (cognitive trails) by which energy can flow faster, more efficiently, and with a strong electromagnetic signal.

At its core, RAS acts as a filter for your awareness. By visualizing more, you expand your awareness, which in turn enhances your capacity for higher consciousness. This increased awareness is crucial for successful visualization. Here's where the RAS and the pineal gland intersect: they both function as gatekeepers in your mind and body, often more focused on protection than on liberation. These systems can sometimes restrict us, holding us back from our full potential. Mastering your manifestation skills involves learning how to navigate these internal gateways. It's about moving beyond them when necessary, using your RAS to effectively synthesize information and your pineal gland to transcend it. Training these parts of your brain to work in your favour can unlock many barriers that stand in your way.

To effectively utilize this knowledge, start by visualizing what you want. Immerse yourself in the emotions of having achieved your goals. Energize and resonate with these experiences.

This is where my Qi Life technologies come into play. While there are many traditional methods to enhance your RAS and activate your pineal gland—such as deep meditation, reading relevant materials, practicing gratitude and forgiveness, and engaging with like-minded individuals—automating these processes represents the future of manifestation. Automated systems make the practice of manifesting effortless, time-efficient, safe, targeted, and personalized, as well as cost-effective and convenient. These technologies are designed to support your journey towards unlocking your potential, backed by science to enhance and streamline the process of achieving your goals.

For decades, researchers have discovered that the pineal gland contains tissues and fluids that are *piezoelectric*, meaning they can generate an electric charge when pressured or heated. This characteristic is also found in other biological materials like bone, DNA, and proteins. Notably, the pineal gland includes calcified deposits similar to bone minerals, which researchers believe could impact its sensitivity to electromagnetic fields (Lang, 1996; Holler, 2007). This sensitivity is why you might hear about "decalcifying your third eye" as part of efforts to awaken the pineal gland. Chemical engineer Sidney Lang explored whether changes in the electromagnetic resonance of the pineal gland could trigger internal messengers that create new regulations in the brain and body. His research confirmed that the pineal gland is significantly more responsive to piezoelectric effects compared to non-pineal tissues, suggesting it acts as a gateway for frequencies to transform the mind due to its high receptivity to external inputs (Lang, 1996).

Building on these findings, biophysicist Simon Baconnier worked with Lang to identify unique piezoelectric properties in the pineal gland. They discovered a specific type of crystal responsible for an "electromechanical biological transduction mechanism," making the gland particularly sensitive to various frequency ranges. This sensitivity allows for morphological changes within the gland depending on the frequency, which can alter its cellular environment and potentially the entire cellular membrane of related cells (Baconnier, 2002). Essentially, frequency input can modify how the pineal gland functions, proving that these microcrystals, or pinealocytes, can *communicate* and activate broader brain regions around the gland. This groundbreaking work highlights the pineal gland's critical role as an interface between external energies and the brain's internal processes.

At Qi Life, we use technology that employs targeted frequencies specifically designed to resonate with various aspects of abundance, from wealth to love. These frequencies help align your energy systems with the universe's abundance, creating an environment where prosperity flourishes. Our technology is designed to activate the pineal gland and program the Reticular Activating System (RAS) to work in the background, tuning them to function on autopilot. This allows you to elevate your energy and perceive information beyond the normal capacity of the five senses. Using our technology can lead you towards achieving a *luminous* mind, or 'samadhi', as described in the meditation traditions of Buddhism, Hinduism, and Sikhism. You can start this journey with our Qi Coil™ devices that use low-frequency electromagnetic waves and are both non-invasive and contactless, immersing you in the right frequencies to activate your pineal gland. We've developed specific frequencies that target the pineal gland, such as our Pineal Gland Activation frequency, which is available for free at members.Qi-Coil.com. Additionally, we also have DMT frequencies that emulate the effects of the spirit molecule, and Ayahuasca frequencies for a safe spiritual awakening experience. These special frequencies allow you to experience profound spiritual insights without the side effects commonly associated with physical substances, which can be hard to access and may pose risks. You can explore more about these transformative options in our Spiritual Awakening Frequency Collection at QiLifeStore.com.

Many of our users have had spiritual awakenings or other profound spiritual experiences. Dr. Har Hari, a chiropractor, shared a captivating account of how his energy levels dramatically increased after using his Qi Coil™. He noted that within just 30 seconds of activating the device, he felt a significant shift in his energy. This surge was so intense that despite having exercised in the morning, he felt compelled to keep moving and engaging in activities because his body was brimming with energy.

Another user, Vanessa, described a profound spiritual journey facilitated by her Qi Coil™. According to her, the device transported her beyond the usual bounds of reality. She reported feeling as if she was not in this dimension or realm at all, suggesting a deep, transcendental experience. Both of these stories illustrate the unique and powerful impact of our coil devices on users' spiritual lives, offering them extraordinary experiences of energy and transcendence.

By opening your third eye and enhancing your awareness, you can tap into the true power of your mind, making personal transformation an automated and easily built upon process. You'll gain the ability to *create* your own reality by transcending into a higher spiritual space and becoming proficient in seeing beyond the physical realm. This aligns with what René Descartes referred to when he described the pineal gland as the 'seat of the soul'. At Qi Life, we bridge the gap between ancient wisdom and modern science, providing you with the knowledge and practical tools to embark on this transformative journey. The pineal gland, located at the centre of your brain, is your personal gateway to higher consciousness—you just need the right resources and confidence to walk through it.

CHAPTER 5
THE FREQUENCY-EMOTION CONNECTION

I n this chapter, we'll delve deeper into the complex relationship between emotions and frequencies. Emotions are the canvas upon which the events of our lives are painted, and understanding how they influence our overall frequency is crucial for personal transformation.

We've already introduced this topic in previous chapters, but now we aim to explore it more thoroughly. We'll examine the emotional spectrum, from the lower vibrational states such as fear and anger to the higher frequencies associated with love and joy. Each emotion emits its own unique energy signature, and recognizing where you fall on this spectrum is the first step towards transforming your life.

THE "EMOTIONAL GUIDANCE SCALE" AND MANIFESTATION

The 'Emotional Guidance Scale' is a powerful tool for understanding how our emotions impact our ability to manifest desires. Popularized within the Law of Attraction community, this scale helps you pinpoint where your emotions lie and how you can shift them to better align with what you wish to achieve.

Introduced by Esther and Jerry Hicks, the Emotional Guidance Scale serves as a navigational aid for exploring your emotional range, with the goal of attracting more positive experiences into your life. The core idea is that our emotions reflect our vibrational alignment with the universe. Higher emotions on the scale signify alignment with positive energy, making you more receptive to favourable outcomes. Conversely, emotions lower on the scale correlate with less desirable experiences. Using this scale, you can become more aware of your current emotional state. This awareness enables you to consciously adjust your thoughts and actions to elevate your emotions, thereby increasing your vibrational frequency. The scale categorizes common emotional states, providing a framework for understanding and improving your emotional well-being. By actively managing your emotions through this scale, you can empower yourself to make deliberate choices that enhance your overall mindset and attract the positive changes you seek (Hicks, 2004).

The scale has 22 emotional states and orders them from highest vibration to lowest vibration. Let's look at the emotions in that order...

1. Joy / Appreciation / Empowered / Freedom / Love
2. Passion
3. Enthusiasm / Eagerness / Happiness
4. Positive Expectation / Belief
5. Optimism
6. Hopefulness
7. Satisfaction / Contentment
8. Boredom
9. Pessimism
10. Frustration / Irritation / Impatience
11. Overwhelmed
12. Disappointment
13. Doubt
14. Worry
15. Blame
16. Discouragement
17. Anger

18. Revenge
19. Hatred / Rage
20. Jealousy
21. Insecurity / Guilt / Unworthiness
22. Fear / Grief / Depression / Despair / Powerlessness

The Emotional Guidance Scale organizes emotional states in a clear hierarchy, helping you understand their impact on your personal energy field. Recognizing where your current state of mind sits on this scale can be transformative. Here's how:

1. **Understand your emotions:** Being able to identify and label your emotions as they occur is crucial. This understanding helps you recognize what you are feeling and why, enhancing your emotional intelligence.
2. **Make conscious choices:** Once you've identified your emotions, you gain the ability to decide how you want to respond to them. Labeling your feelings gives you the power to shift your emotional state to better match your desires.
3. **Align with positive energy:** Choosing higher vibrational emotions allows you to align your personal energy field with positive frequencies. This alignment makes you a stronger receptor for positive experiences and relationships.
4. **Increase your emotional well-being:** Actively recognizing and engaging with your emotions promotes the cultivation of higher vibrational states, enhancing your life's overall fulfillment and happiness.
5. **Manifest your desires:** According to the Law of Attraction, the energy you emit is the energy you attract. By aligning your emotions with your desires, you enhance your receptivity to the outcomes you most want.
6. **Achieve personal growth and empowerment:** The scale challenges you to become proactive about your emotional states. By increasing your emotional awareness, you can preemptively manage your emotions rather than being controlled by them. This proactive approach helps you

mitigate negative emotions that lower your vibrational energy, giving you control over your emotional journey with intentional and purposeful actions.

The Emotional Guidance Scale is not about suppressing or ignoring lower vibrational emotions, which can be valid and useful in the right contexts. Instead, it's about empowering you to discern when these emotions serve you and when they do not. Utilizing the scale effectively involves understanding when and how to harness both positive and negative emotions to your benefit. Let's explore how you can leverage this scale to maximize its advantages in your life.

Emotional Guidance Scale:

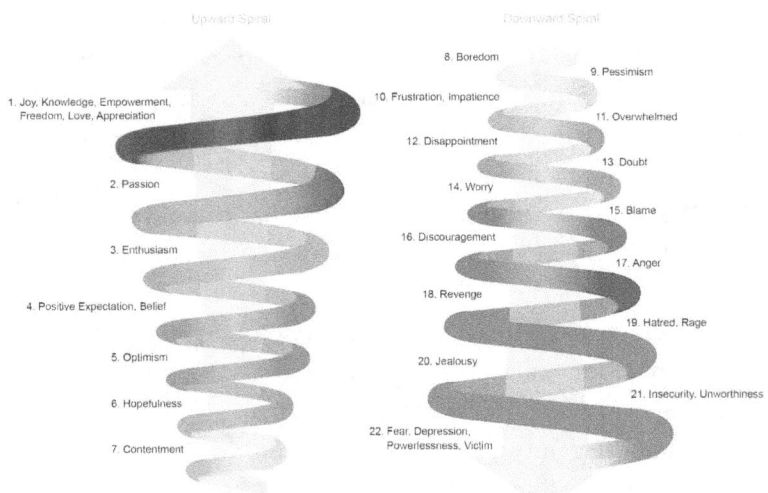

Upward Spiral

Downward Spiral

1. Joy, Knowledge, Empowerment, Freedom, Love, Appreciation

2. Passion

3. Enthusiasm

4. Positive Expectation, Belief

5. Optimism

6. Hopefulness

7. Contentment

8. Boredom

9. Pessimism

10. Frustration, Impatience

11. Overwhelmed

12. Disappointment

13. Doubt

14. Worry

15. Blame

16. Discouragement

17. Anger

18. Revenge

19. Hatred, Rage

20. Jealousy

21. Insecurity, Unworthiness

22. Fear, Depression, Powerlessness, Victim

HOW TO RAISE YOUR EMOTIONAL FREQUENCY

Raising your emotional frequency isn't just a lofty concept. It's an actionable process with real-world implications. While straightforward, identifying your emotional state and where you fit on the Emotional Guidance Scale requires true honesty with yourself. Only through genuine self-reflection and purposeful introspection can you shift your emotional state to a higher vibrational range.

To start, you need to accurately identify your current emotional state. What feelings are dominant for you right now? Recognizing your emotions sounds simple, but it often isn't. You may be asking: How can I move up the scale?

Moving up the scale involves considering thoughts or actions that could elevate you to a higher emotional frequency. For example, if you're feeling anger, practicing gratitude or engaging in a calming activity might help. This deliberate intentionality is key to elevating your frequency. Regularly taking stock of your emotional state can improve your ability to shift your emotions. Take a few moments throughout your day to consider and reflect on your feelings. How can I reframe the negativity I'm experiencing? What kind of self-care can I engage in right now? What would bring me joy in this moment? It's important to be kind to yourself if you're experiencing lower vibrational states. The Emotional Guidance Scale isn't about self-criticism; it's a tool for facilitating progressive improvement until managing your emotions feels more natural and automatic.

The Hicks offer a selection of activities that can aid in your vibrational elevation. They include:

1. **Conscious awareness:** Take a moment to identify your current emotional state. Awareness grants recognition. Recognition enables the power to change.
2. **Thought reframing:** Challenge your limiting, lower vibrational feelings and reframe them. Allow your inner monologue to speak positively about yourself and what you're doing. Engage in positive affirmations.
3. **Practice gratitude:** When you're in a lower vibrational state, think about what you're grateful for rather than what's holding you back. Focussing on the positives in your life raises your frequency.
4. **Meditate and visualize:** Picture what it is you desire in your mind's eye. Produce a clear mental image of what you want and how you wish to feel. Consider the emotions you wish

to experience and imagine yourself experiencing them as clearly as you can. Engage in meditative acts to calm your mind and alleviate stress. Relaxation can often be the first step to emotional clarity.

5. **Engage in joy:** What sort of activities, hobbies, or pastimes bring you joy—particularly simple ones that you can easily engage in on a regular basis? Do something creative. Exercise. Get outside for a walk. Put on some music that makes you want to dance. Call or meet someone who makes you smile.

6. **Practice self-care:** It's the simple self-care activities that can make the most astounding difference in your life. Go to bed earlier. Eat healthier foods. Set boundaries. Take a moment to recharge when you need to.

7. **Surround yourself with positivity:** The people and experiences you engage with day-to-day will have the greatest external impact on you, so make sure to surround yourself with people and things that exude positivity. Prioritize relationships that add to your life rather than subtract from it. Say no to activities that bring your spirits down whenever you can.

8. **Let go and forgive:** Don't hold grudges. A grudge is an emotional roadblock. It holds you back from pushing forward into positivity. When something weighs on you emotionally (be it due to your own actions or someone else's), find the quickest path to forgiveness and move on.

Implementing these steps effectively involves setting regular reminders to check in with yourself about your current emotional state and pinpointing where you fall on the Emotional Guidance Scale. These reminders encourage strong habits of self-reflection and recognition. Keeping a gratitude journal is another practical way to track your feelings and the reasons behind them. It's also crucial to celebrate your emotional victories. For example, if you start the week feeling low but manage to elevate your emotional state by the weekend, take time to appreciate this progress and reward yourself accordingly. Rewarding yourself for emotional growth reinforces positive changes and encourages more consistent, higher vibrational states. Being in control of your feelings means you can truly achieve emotional freedom. As Esther and Jerry Hicks have pointed out, "The basis of life is freedom; the purpose of life is joy; the result of life is growth."

DECODING THE FREQUENCY BEHIND YOUR FEELINGS

"The mind most effectually works upon the body, producing by his passions and perturbations miraculous alterations . . . cruel diseases and sometimes death itself." — Robert Burton The Anatomy of Melancholy, 1621

Raising your vibrational energy is crucial for more than just mental well-being; it's a biological necessity that affects every part of your body. Research confirms that emotions influence not only the brain but also your overall physical health, impacting cognitive functions, hormonal balance, immune response, and much more.

A significant study from 2006 highlighted how emotions play a critical role in the onset or progression of major illnesses such as cancer, HIV, cardiovascular diseases, and autoimmune disorders. It found that individuals with a predominantly negative emotional style have a weaker immune response, which can increase their risk of illness compared to those with a positive emotional outlook (Barak, 2006). Further research by scientists at the London School of Medicine has shown that the immune system is not only affected by the physical environment but also by the social environment, which includes emotional contexts. This research has even demonstrated that emotions can influence the effectiveness of medications. For instance, the social context surrounding patients with psychiatric disorders can significantly affect the outcomes of their pharmacological treatments. Much like a placebo can create a positive mental state that leads to health benefits, a positive mindset can enhance the effectiveness of actual medications. These findings reinforce the notion that "happiness and healthiness go hand in hand" (Brod, 2014).

The link between emotional well-being and bodily functions is profound and supported by an increasing body of research. For instance, a 2023 study highlighted that positive emotions correlate with lower inflammation levels and a more robust antiviral gene expression, while negative emotions tend to increase inflammation and dampen antiviral responses. This research underlines a clear biological pathway where cultivating a positive emotional state can significantly benefit immune system functionality, particularly in adolescents, who experience emotions more intensely than adults and younger children (Rahal, 2023).

Beyond immune responses, emotional well-being impacts other critical health areas. Historical data suggests that negative emotional states can enhance and prolong cardiovascular activation, which may lead to heart disease (Blascovich, 1993). Conversely, positive emotions have been associated with reductions in blood pressure and hypertension risks (Blumenthal, 1985). Longitudinal studies have further established that individuals who consistently experienced positive emotions from childhood into adulthood show markedly less cumulative wear and tear on their bodies compared to others (Ryff, in press). Moreover, positivity has been linked to practical health outcomes such as a decreased likelihood of disablement and an increased lifespan (Ostir, 2000). There's also emerging evidence suggesting that severe emotional distress from adverse life events like isolation, abuse, or loss might leave a 'genetic signature' that impacts the immune system (D'Acquisto, 2017).

The relationship between emotional well-being and brain health is compellingly demonstrated by various studies that highlight how emotions impact cognitive functioning. For instance, a 2017 study involving multiple universities across China discovered that positive emotions significantly boost cognitive flexibility, enabling individuals to switch more smoothly between different tasks (Wang, 2017). This flexibility is partly attributed to increased levels of brain dopamine, a neurotransmitter that enhances the brain's ability to modulate attention across different tasks (Ashby, 1999). The study by Wang further notes that positive emotions not only improve cognitive control but also reduce the activation of brain areas associated with conflict, streamlining cognitive processes. Conversely, negative emotions have a detrimental effect on the brain's ability to focus. Research has shown that negative states drain cognitive resources, undermining the ability to maintain attention on tasks (Meinhardt, 2003). This lack of 'attentional control' is evident in individuals experiencing negative emotions, as they struggle to perform even basic tasks efficiently. The impact of emotions on cognitive functions is also evident in studies of depression. Individuals suffering from depression often report a decreased ability to carry out day-to-day activities or to maintain focus on tasks, a condition tied to diminished positive emotions. The reduction in positive emotions impairs executive functions necessary for planning, problem-solving, and participating in active tasks (Yin, 2019).

The 'broaden-and-build theory' proposed by Barbara Fredrickson is a significant concept in understanding the impact of emotions on neurological functions. This theory suggests that positive emotions do more than just make us feel good temporarily; they also contribute to long-term personal growth and social connectivity. According to Fredrickson, positive emotions expand our awareness and build enduring personal and social resources, transforming us for the better and enhancing our future lives (Fredrickson, 2001). Fredrickson's research indicates that experiencing emotions such as joy, interest, contentment, and love not only helps diminish persistent negative feelings but also boosts psychological resilience. This enhanced resilience facilitates upward spirals of emotional and cognitive improvement, leading to a richer, more fulfilling life (Fredrickson, 1998, 2000).

Furthering this idea, a 2020 study demonstrated that the brain networks responsible for implementing positive emotions are notably more adaptable and capable of modification than those associated with negative emotions. The study found that positive stimuli foster a beneficial link between cognitive systems and the peripheral nervous system (Alexander, 2020). In practical terms, this means that a general state of contentment makes our brains more open to growth, more receptive to new ideas, and better equipped to tackle problem-solving, multitasking, and challenges. As a result, there is an enhancement in the formation of new neural pathways, increased neuroplasticity, and a heightened ability to manifest desired outcomes.

As we come to a close on our scientific exploration in this chapter, let's consider an extraordinary national endeavour in Bhutan, a small country nestled between China and India. The Bhutanese government has embarked on a mission to enhance the overall happiness of its citizens by improving access to essential services such as clean water, sanitation, electricity, and education. By alleviating deprivation in these key areas, they aim to boost the emotional well-being of the population (Nidup, 2017). Bhutan's approach is deeply influenced by its Buddhist cultural roots, which emphasize spirituality and compassion. The nation integrates mindfulness into everyday life, focusing on mental health alongside economic factors. This holistic approach demonstrates that prioritizing positive, high vibrational energy can manifest better societal outcomes. This national strategy serves as a macro-level illustration of the principles we've discussed on a micro-level throughout this chapter.

This sort of real-world case study is something we at Qi Life have been exploring ourselves. Much like Carol Dweck's work with students, which I covered in Chapter Three, Qi Life has been exploring the power of frequency on emotional and cognitive well-being in educational settings. One school that we partnered with integrated Qi Coil™ frequencies into the curriculum of its lowest performing class. This class consisted of students labeled with ADHD, autism, and various learning disabilities whose difficulty regulating their emotions frequently got in the way of their studies.

In just four months, these students experienced profound changes. One struggling fourth-grade student scored a 245 on his math assessment, a score average for a twelfth-grader. Another second-grader began solving complex addition problems, a task usually expected of fifth graders and beyond. One student mastered complex division and even began teaching fellow classmates. Concentration rates and the ability to engage confidently with the material and each other rose markedly. Previously, their attention span might have been as short as nine seconds, but with the help of Qi Coils™, these kids found new focus and enthusiasm for learning—overcoming their educational and emotional hurdles, and moving from the bottom 20% to achieving scores in the top 1%!

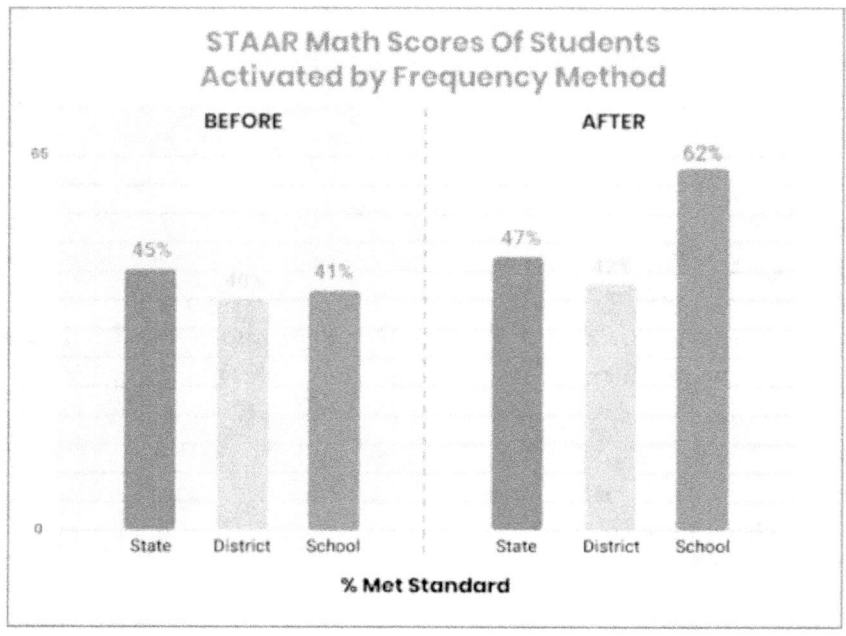

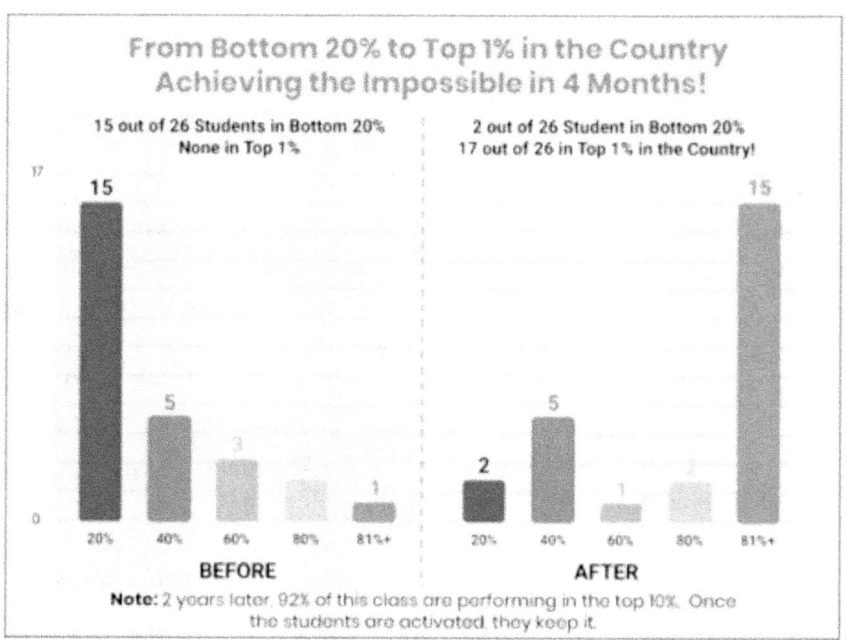

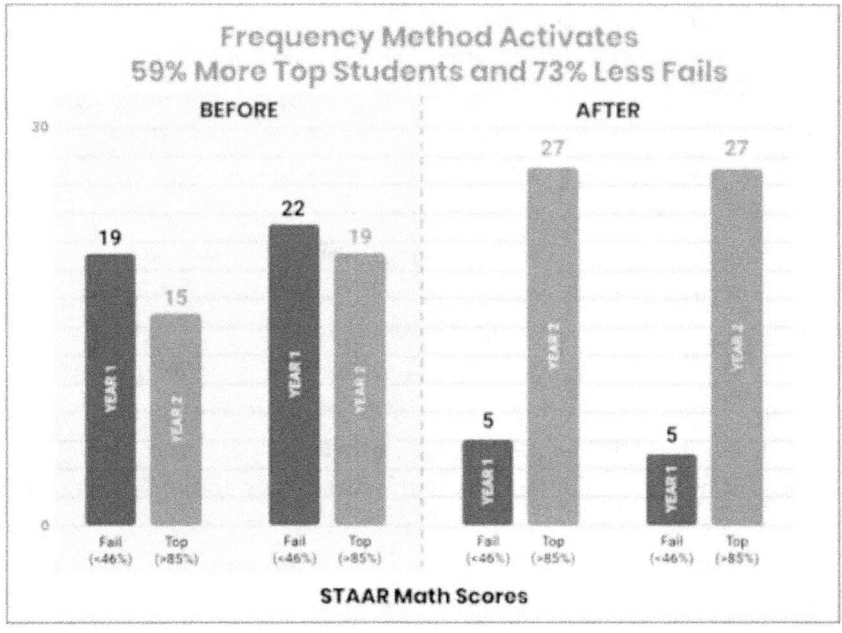

Frequency Method Activates
59% More Top Students and 73% Less Fails

STAAR Math Scores

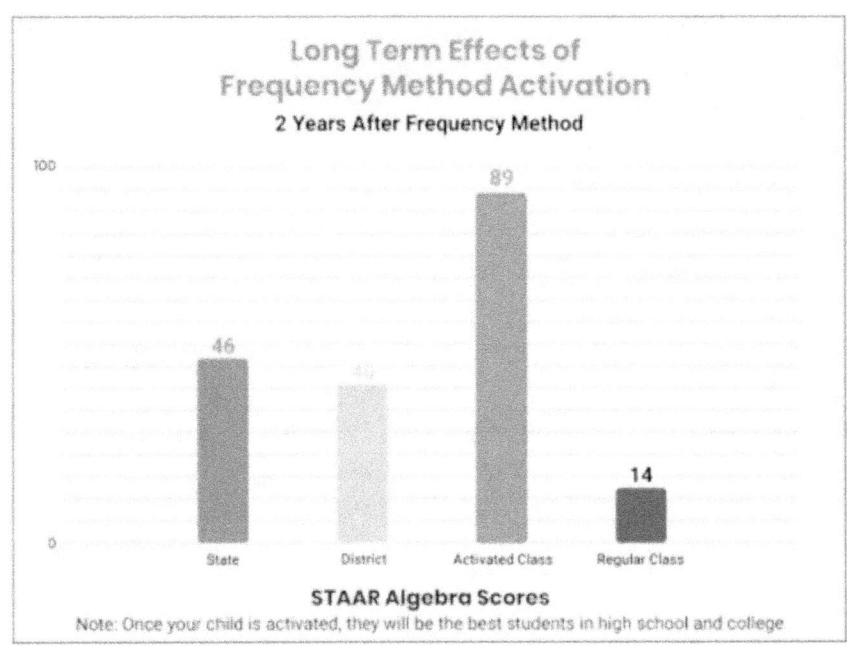

Long Term Effects of
Frequency Method Activation

2 Years After Frequency Method

STAAR Algebra Scores

Note: Once your child is activated, they will be the best students in high school and college

These success stories underscore the potential of frequency modulation to fundamentally elevate a person's emotional and cognitive energy, moving away from traditional pharmaceutical interventions, which often have lasting negative impacts. This approach is not only limited to education, Qi Coils™ are currently being explored in clinical trials at psychiatric clinics for treating depression, mental and emotional disorders, PTSD, and addiction. The trials are showing promising results in improving mental health conditions without the use of drugs and with minimal coaching.

This approach taps into our core emotional and mental frequencies, offering a smarter, non-invasive way to enhance our well-being. By using Qi Coils™, we're enabling individuals to boost their mental and emotional health fundamentally, without resorting to medications and with minimal intervention. It's a practical and modern method that resonates particularly well with those seeking straightforward, effective solutions in their busy lives. For more insights and information on how these frequencies are solving ADHD, autism spectrum disorder, PTSD and other mental health problems, be sure to visit Frequency-Method.com.

In summation, by raising your emotional frequency, you can manifest your desires with greater clarity, intention, and precision. Achieving this requires a holistic view of ourselves, taking into account the mind, body, brain, soul, and spirit. Each aspect of our being is interconnected through energy and frequency, influencing our overall health and capacity for achieving our goals. Fulvio D'Acquisto from the London School of Medicine, whose work highlights the impact of emotions on health, cites a Jain parable to emphasize the importance of considering the whole when examining the parts of something...

Once upon a time, there lived six blind men in a village. One day the villagers told them, "Hey, there is an elephant in the village today. They had no idea what an elephant was. They decided "Even though we would not be able to see it, let us go and feel it anyway." All of them went to where the elephant was.

Every one of them touched the elephant.

"Hey, the elephant is a pillar," said the first man, who touched his leg. "Oh, no! it is like a rope," said the second man, who touched the tail. "Oh, no!

it is like a thick branch of a tree," said the third man, who touched the trunk of the elephant. "It is like a big hand fan" said the fourth man, who touched the ear of the elephant. "It is like a huge wall," said the fifth man, who touched the belly of the elephant. "It is like a solid pipe," Said the sixth man, who touched the tusk of the elephant.

They began to argue about the elephant and every one of them insisted that he was right. It looked as if they were getting agitated. A wise man was passing by and he saw this he stopped and asked them, "What is the matter?" They said, "We cannot agree to what the elephant is like." Each one of them told what he thought the elephant was like. The wise man calmly explained to them, "All of you are right. The reason every one of you is telling it differently is because each one of you touched a different part of the elephant. So, actually the elephant has all the features that each of you mentioned.

I share this story as it demonstrates yet another example of ancient wisdom. It's a reminder of how crucial it is to step back and recognize the interconnectedness of everything. Like the villagers who could not perceive the elephant's true form because they focused on individual parts, we too can become blind to our true selves by separating the cognitive from the physical. Both are expressions of the same energy flows—whether they are in balance or imbalance, harmony or discord. Understanding yourself holistically is essential for manifesting what you want in life. Don't just see the parts; see the whole. By raising your emotional vibrational energy, you also elevate your physical vibrational energy. This alignment allows you to achieve your goals more effectively. Change your frequency, change your destiny.

CHAPTER 6
THE LAW OF ATTRACTION: AUTOMATED

Unless you've been living under a rock, you've no doubt heard of the Law of Attraction. Its basic premise is straightforward: what you put out into the universe is what you get back. Like attracts like. But what you might not realize is that this theory is far more complex than it seems. In this chapter, we'll take a deep dive into the Law of Attraction—how it's truly a frequency-driven universal law, considered by some to be the most powerful of the universal laws (Hicks, 2006).

Let's start with some basics. The Law of Attraction, when actively engaged in manifesting, is about bringing into your life what you most desire through intentional thoughts and desires—essentially, creating your own reality (Losier, 2006). Every thought we have generates a vibration or frequency that extends out into the world. Vibrations that match your frequency naturally resonate back to you. The key is to align your energy with the universe's energy to attract what you desire. Think of it as similar to the principle of cause and effect, or reaping what you sow.

This concept of 'give and receive' is an ancient one. The Bible is full of verses that allude to the same ideas and concepts:

- **(Matthew 21:22)** *"And all things, whatsoever you shall ask in prayer, believing, you shall receive."*
- **(Mark 11:24)** *"Therefore I tell you, whatever you ask for in prayer, believe that you have received it, and it will be yours."*
- **(Matthew 7:7)** *"Ask, and it shall be given to you; seek, and you shall find; knock, and it shall be opened unto you."*
- **(Mark 9:23)** *"If thou can believe, all things are possible, to him that believeth."*
- **(Proverbs 23:7)** *"As a man thinks in his heart, so is he."*
- **(Romans 12:2)** *"Do not conform to the pattern of this world, but be transformed, by the renewing of your mind."*
- **(Corinthians 4:18)** *"Fix your eyes not on what is seen, but on what is unseen, since what is seen is temporary, but what is unseen is eternal."*
- **(Mark 11:24)** *"Believe that you have received it, and it will be yours."*

All these ideas represent intentional output to achieve a desired outcome. **Change your frequency, change your destiny**. Ask the universe for what you desire, and it can provide.

This concept isn't unique to Christian scripture. Chinese culture, for example, echoes this sentiment. The ancient philosopher Lao Tzu once said, "Watch your thoughts, they become your words; watch your words, they become your actions; watch your actions, they become your habits; watch your habits, they become your character; watch your character, it becomes your destiny." Similar principles appear throughout Buddhist, Taoist, and Confucian texts. Buddhism particularly emphasizes that both positive and negative thoughts and deeds will eventually return to you and those around you. A story from the 1600s about Yuan Liaofan, who wrote to his son on how to create his own destiny in what became known as *Liaofan's Four Lessons*, underscores this idea, suggesting that both good fortune and bad fortune originate from within oneself (Zhang, 2017).

In Hinduism, the concept of *karma*, or the Law of Action, aligns closely with this idea. It holds that one must perform their worldly duties with clear visualization (*mansa*), affirmative speech (*vacha*), and physical involvement (*karmana*) (Pathak, 2023). The Bhagavad Gita teaches that your deeds will result in reciprocal impacts from the universe, and Hindu teachings suggest that your actions in this life will affect you in your next life, an idea encapsulated in the Law of Manu. Karma is intertwined with the Law of Attraction, particularly through the concept of *sankalpa*—or intention—which promotes acting with detachment from outcomes. To attract positive experiences, one must act positively for its own sake, not merely in anticipation of a reward.

Finally, let's look briefly at Islam. In Islamic teachings, the Law of Attraction is equally present. Allah says, "If you give thanks, I will give you more" (Quran 14:7), promoting the practice of gratitude, a fundamental aspect of the Law of Attraction. Muslims have long embraced the power of manifestation by acknowledging and appreciating the goodness and blessings in life. Another passage states, "Surely Allah does not change the conditions in which a people are in until they change that which is in themselves" (Quran 13:11), supporting the idea that you receive from the universe what you emit into it. Islam also aligns with the concept of universal frequency or cosmic/divine energy, as represented by Allah. The Quran teaches that everything happens through Allah, emphasizing our connection to a universal energy. Aligning with this energy means harmonizing your own energies to resonate with divine will.

As we can see, ancient traditions from around the world reflect the Law of Attraction in diverse yet fundamentally similar ways. They all converge on the principle that like attracts like, mediated by a universal energy or divine essence. To tap into this force, you must first align your own energies. It's about turning your mind and body into receivers for the destiny you aim to craft. The process involves three key steps: Attract, Ask, and Allow. These are essential components of the Law of Attraction that help you engage with this universal law effectively. Let's break them down further...

1. **Attract:** your thoughts and feelings are electromagnetic. They will attract similar energy, *therefore, practice:*
2. **Ask/Create:** you must ask in order to create. You must be

aware of your thoughts in order to consciously manifest them. Creation is a deliberate process.

3. **Allow:** you must be open to receiving the creations of your manifesting. You must not worry about, resist, or block the energy coming your way.

The second step is critical to proper allowance and attraction. There must be intention to your *ask* of the universe. You must actively and consciously focus on positive thoughts to generate positive energy. Over time, this practice becomes habitual, and the positive frequency you emit will become automated. Most of us deal with thousands of negative thoughts daily, often driven by ego and fear (Tolle, 2005). By recognizing and transforming these energies, you position yourself to better receive—or *allow*—more positive energies in return. Essentially, by asking for what you desire, you generate the energy necessary to attract it (Braden, 2008). This transformation involves dissipating ego-driven and fearful thoughts, freeing you to manifest your desires (Chopra, 2004).

To summarize, when you request what you want, you create the positive thoughts and feelings—the frequency—that enables you to allow (attract or receive) what you asked for into your life. With intentional practice, this process can unfold naturally (Mullins, 2008).

However, the practice of *allowing* can often be the most challenging part. Why is this? It primarily involves letting go, which is more of a subconscious effort—an absence of negative thoughts and energy where doubt doesn't cloud the mind. Doubt often stems from limiting beliefs about oneself, which can restrict or even completely block what you're trying to attract. Research supports this; for instance, a Duke University study found that stress and negative emotions can increase heart rate and sour mood (Merritt, 1999). A useful approach to enhancing your ability to allow and receive is to detach from the outcome of what you're asking for. Instead of focusing on the outcome, concentrate on your output. As the Beatles famously sang, "let it be." When you let experiences unfold without fretting about their outcomes, you increase your capacity to *allow*, making you more receptive to the energies needed to realize your ambitions fully.

Tony Robbins, a renowned life coach, argues that our minds naturally condition our future based on past experiences. He suggests that by interrupting these limiting thoughts, we can break free from the patterns that hold us back (Robbins, 1989).

Additionally, there are three core principles often highlighted by advocates of the Law of Attraction that align closely with the distinctions previously mentioned:

1. **Like Attracts Like:** This principle echoes much of what we've discussed. It suggests that similar things attract each other, including people and thoughts. Thus, negativity attracts negative outcomes, while positivity draws in desirable results and experiences.
2. **Nature Abhors a Vacuum:** According to this principle, removing negative thoughts and feelings creates space for new ones to emerge. Since it's impossible for the brain to exist in a neutral or *empty* state, when you discard negativity, it's crucial to consciously fill that space with positivity.
3. **The Present is Always Perfect:** This principle encourages active participation in the present moment. Rather than focusing on dread, worry, or unhappiness, it suggests channeling energy into making the present as fulfilling as

possible, often through practices like gratitude and intentionality.

The idea of *crafting* the present moment is particularly powerful and something we'll touch on later in this chapter.

BEYOND VISUALIZATION: ACTIVATING THE LAW OF ATTRACTION THROUGH FREQUENCY

The scientific foundation for the Law of Attraction includes fascinating insights from the field of neuroscience. Consider the behaviour of electrons within our atoms: they are constantly vibrating and, when aligned, create an electromagnetic force. This suggests that every atom in our bodies is continually responding to external energy inputs (Losier, 2006).

A pivotal discovery that supports this idea occurred in the mid-1990s by Italian researchers at the University of Parma. During experiments involving electrode implants in monkeys, researchers noticed that the monkeys' premotor cortices showed bursts of activity not only when the monkeys held a piece of food but also when they observed scientists handling food. This dual activation during both direct action (holding food) and perception (seeing someone else with food) led to the identification of what are now known as 'mirror neurons'. The implication of mirror neurons is profound: they suggest that the same brain regions involved in performing an action are also activated by seeing that action performed by others. According to Günther Knoblich of Rutgers University, this discovery indicates that "the same brain region that controls action also supports perception." Thus, our brains engage with and respond to our environment in ways deeply influenced by social interactions. This means what we emit in terms of actions and emotions can resonate and be mirrored by those around us, highlighting a fundamental aspect of human cognition—our interconnectedness through shared experiences and responses (Jaffe, 2007).

When you last witnessed someone get injured, did you flinch as if you felt their pain? That type of *reflective* response is your mirror neurons in action. They allow your brain to interpret and empathize with others' experiences by mimicking what you see. This mechanism is why we can often feel a physical response when we see someone else suffering. This same principle helps explain how infants learn from their environment. According to developmental psychologist Andrew Meltzoff from the University of Washington, infants can start imitating behaviours they observe within weeks of birth. Their brains use mirror neurons to bridge the gap between seeing an action and performing it themselves. This isn't just a phenomenon observed in humans but is a basic principle of learning observed across many species, often described as "monkey see, monkey do" or in our case, "baby see, baby do."

Jean Decety of the University of Chicago highlights how this ties into the Law of Attraction, explaining that our desire strongly influences our brain's perception-action system to recognize and pursue elements in our environment that fulfill our wants and needs (Jaffe, 2007). In essence, when you focus on and emit positive intentions and energy, the brains of those around you notice and can mirror this positive behaviour. This mirroring can lead to a shared uplift in mood and motivation, showing how deeply interconnected our emotions and actions are with those around us. So, when you smile or witness joy, such as a baby laughing, it can instantly elevate your mood because your neurons are reflecting the positive signals they detect from others and vice versa.

Research shows that our actions and emotional expressions can influence others due to the function of mirror neurons. These neurons activate not only when we perform an action but also when we observe the same action in others. This concept is rooted in the famous philosophical statement "I think, therefore I am," suggesting that our behaviours can transform our environment to reflect our intentions. For example, one study demonstrated how mirror neurons link different sensory inputs from our environment (Acharya, 2012). In a fascinating experiment, one group of participants was exposed to unpleasant odours while another group only watched videos of the first group's reactions, which typically involved scrunched noses and squinty eyes. The brain areas responsible for processing smells, specifically the anterior insula and cingulate cortex, were active in the first group experiencing the bad smells directly. Remarkably, these same brain areas also activated in the second group, who only observed the reactions without smelling the odours themselves (Wicker, 2003). This study, along with others, shows that emotions can trigger specific neural circuits, and merely observing these emotions can activate the same circuits in others.

The energy we emit is often *mirrored back* to us. "Anxious people tend to make others around them anxious, and the same goes for fear and other emotions. Conversely, happiness and anticipation of rewards can light up those same emotional centres in others," explains Harvard professor of psychiatry Srinivasan Pillay, who highlights that the parts of the brain responsible for forming intentions are closely connected to those that govern actions. This implies that if others reflect our emotions and behaviours, they can also reflect our intentions, creating a kind of emotional contagion. "The intensity of our emotions and actions plays a crucial role in drawing what we desire into our lives," Pillay notes. (Pillay, 2011)

WHY GRATITUDE IS THE KEY TO MANIFESTING YOUR DREAMS

As I mentioned earlier, gratitude and intentionality are key to effectively using the Law of Attraction to achieve your goals. These practices set the right conditions for attracting what you want. Now, let's explore some essential methods to integrate the Law of Attraction into your daily life and shape your present reality:

- Be grateful
- Visualize your desires
- Look for silver linings
- Identify negative feelings
- Use positive affirmation
- Reframe negativity

These methods can build strong habits and assist in cultivating optimism in your daily routine. They also enhance motivation as you pursue your goals. As Dr. Elizabeth Scott notes, you can apply these methods across different areas of your life—work, personal relationships, and finances. At work, concentrate on making small positive changes that advance your career, like learning new skills or aiming for promotions. In your personal life, address any negative feelings towards others by trying to understand different perspectives and being more open. For your financial health, move away from a scarcity mindset and focus on abundance—appreciate what you have instead of fixating on what you lack (Scott, 2024).

Gratitude and setting intentions work best together. Integrate intentionality into your gratitude. Don't just be thankful for what you have, but also for what you want to attract. Make your gratitude anticipatory, like thanking in advance. Each morning, set a daily intention and express gratitude for the achievements and experiences you aim for that day. Every day offers new opportunities and possibilities. Combining intention with gratitude allows you to feel thankful for future achievements before they occur. Visualize yourself achieving your goals—getting that promotion, meeting a significant other, increasing your income, improving your fitness. By deeply feeling these future successes now, you align your energy with the frequencies needed to turn these desires into reality.

This enhanced focus on intentional gratitude positions you to seize opportunities for wealth, escape stagnation, develop deeper connections, and break free from negative patterns.

- What do you want more of in this life?
- What do you want from your career?
- Which experiences do you want to have?
- What do you want to accomplish?
- How do you want to feel?

These questions can smooth your path to manifesting your desires. They help you set the right intentions and align with the appropriate frequencies.

While actions can create the right frequencies, the frequencies themselves can inspire actions. You can not only attract the right frequency alignment but also enhance the Law of Attraction by immersing yourself in the right frequencies from the start. This involves creating an energy field around you that not only cultivates stronger energy but also protects you from negative energies that surround you daily.

Thousands of people have experienced incredible changes in their lives after trying Qi Coil™, each with a story that highlights its transformative power of abundance attraction. Take Dr. Joe Vitale, for example, a renowned spiritual teacher featured in the movie *The Secret*, recently became acquainted with the Qi Coil™ after interviewing me. During the interview, he asked me which frequency I liked best. I introduced him to the Ultimate Abundance frequency. Intrigued, Joe decided to try this frequency immediately after our conversation. The very next day, to his astonishment, he received an unexpected cheque for $32,000. This unexpected windfall came just after his experiment with the Qi Coil™, turning a normal day into one of unexpected celebration and reinforcing his belief in the power of Qi Coil™. Dr. Vitale now openly advocates for the device, encouraging others to "**Expect Miracles.**"

Sarah, a well known realtor, was looking for ways to expand her client base and decided to use one of Qi Coil's™ frequencies known for enhancing business opportunities. She was skeptical but decided to try it anyway. Just three hours after she started using the technology, she landed a deal that netted her an unexpected $90,000 commission. This new business came through channels she had never tapped into before, showcasing how Qi Coil™ can open new avenues for financial growth.

Kelly, an IT company owner, incorporated the Qi Coil's™ luck frequency into his daily routine, hoping for a positive impact on his business dealings. Remarkably, the very next day, his company closed two deals worth nearly $1,000,000 combined. This rapid success far exceeded his expectations and demonstrated how quickly and powerfully Qi Coil's™ frequencies can influence business outcomes.

Jerome, an entrepreneur drowning in nearly $3 million of debt, was initially skeptical about the potential benefits of Qi Coil™. Desperate for a solution, he finally decided to give it a try. After a few sessions listening to our frequencies, he was struck by a brilliant idea that had been eluding him for a long time. This sudden insight allowed him to formulate a plan to eliminate the $3,000,000 debt entirely! Jerome's turnaround is a testament to how Qi Coil™ can clear mental fog and inspire valuable solutions to seemingly insurmountable problems.

These narratives not only reflect the diverse applications of the Qi Coil™ but also its profound ability to significantly enhance the lives of those who use it, providing not just financial gains but also deep personal insights and solutions.

At Qi Life, our technology surrounds you with the right energy so you can send out stronger signals to the universe and receive more powerful signals in return. Enhancing your energy output can significantly improve your use of the Law of Attraction. You'll feel a deeper connection with the universe, achieve greater joy and fulfillment, and experience more serendipity, good fortune, and success.

CHAPTER 7
SPIRITUAL AWAKENING WITH FREQUENCY

"Then God said, 'Let there be light,' and there was light." This iconic opening from the Bible is familiar to many. Yet, when we pause to deeply consider what these words imply, their significance broadens. This isn't just about the literal emergence of light—it suggests that God's words themselves manifested change. The mere expression brought light into existence where there was none, showcasing the power of divine utterance to alter reality.

Everything in the universe, from the vast galaxies to the minute atoms, vibrates with energy at various frequencies. This universal energy underpins all creation and transformation. Given that everything is essentially energy resonating at specific frequencies, it's not a stretch to think of God's word as a cosmic frequency—a divine energy capable of creating and altering realities. If we accept that God used energy or frequency to shape the world, and if we are indeed created in His image, then perhaps it is also within our capacity, and even our duty, to harness these forms of energy. By understanding and utilizing these cosmic frequencies, we too can influence and transform our own realities.

In this chapter, I will explore the connective tissues that link spirituality with frequency, and how meditation and visualization are the primary means by which to connect and tune into your own spiritual frequency, to fully embrace universal energy to enact your own personal inner transformation.

CONNECTING SPIRITUALITY & FREQUENCY

Ancient civilizations, cultures, and traditions have recognized some form of cosmic energy or frequency. While some cultures were explicit in their descriptions, others used more metaphorical language. Regardless of the approach, they shared a belief in a pervasive energy force often described as a *spirit*.

Most creation narratives from various religious traditions start with a form of spirit or energy that initiates and sustains life. In Christianity, for example, the Holy Spirit moves over the waters of primordial chaos before initiating creation, ultimately giving life to Adam and Eve. This concept, that a divine energy permeates all things, is known as panentheism. Coined by German philosopher Karl Krause in the early 19th century, panentheism suggests that a universal spirit transcends and interpenetrates all aspects of the universe, echoing beliefs held by many ancient faiths like Hinduism (Whiting, 1991; Culp, 2013). This perspective views gods, spirits, and divine energies as interconnected components of this universal force (Kasmer, 2023).

The ancient Greeks also embraced the concept of a unifying cosmic force. Neoplatonist philosophers referred to this singular force as 'the one,' encompassing the divine mind and the cosmic soul. Centuries earlier, the philosopher Heraclitus described a pervasive energy or cosmic law known as the 'logos', implying that all existence is interconnected: "He who hears not me but the logos will say: All is one." More simply put, he who hears not me but **cosmic energy** will say: all is one. Heraclitus also emphasized the perpetual state of change within the universe, famously stating, "Everything flows, nothing stands still."

Similarly, ancient Indian traditions articulate a panentheistic view of the universe. The Rig Veda, dating back to before 1100 BCE, discusses a 'spiritual unity' that pervades the cosmos, where the initial creative impulse of the universe emerges (Nigal, 2009). Advaita Vedanta, a prominent school of Indian philosophy, describes an all-encompassing energy known as 'brahman'—the *ultimate reality* that is indivisible and omnipresent (Southgate, 2011). The Bhagavad Gita further echoes this sentiment in verse IX.4, where Krishna declares, "By Me all this universe is pervaded through My unmanifested form."

Shaktism, commonly associated with Tantra, similarly views 'shakti' as the fundamental cosmic energy—the very foundation of existence and the divine essence that gives rise to the five elements and everything in existence (Subramanian, 1977). These teachings illustrate a profound connection and continuity among various Indian philosophical systems regarding the omnipresence and significance of universal energy.

To circle back to the starting point of this chapter, Christianity also offers insights into a universal energy or spirit. In Colossians 3:11, Paul expresses that God is omnipresent, existing in everything at once. This sentiment echoes through the teachings of American Catholic monk Thomas Keating, who noted that during the Last Supper, Jesus spoke of a profound oneness and about "his intentions to send his Spirit to dwell within us." (Keating, 2012). This indicates that the divine essence, or universal energy, is ever-present within us. The concept of universal energy is further embraced by the Latter-Day Saints who refer to it as the 'Light of Christ'. This energy "proceeds from God through Christ and gives life and light to all things."

In Judaism, we find these references as well. Hasidism speaks of God before the physical manifestation of the universe. This entity or energy force is known as 'Ein Sof', which literally translates to *there is no end*. It has always been present, transcendent, and immanent within all things across space and time (Ariel, 2006).

We can look to Islam to find further support for cosmic energy. The Islamic concept of Wahdat ul-wujud (the Unity of All Things) is described as the conversion of the 'the Unity of Existence' and 'the Unity of Being' (Arts, 2014). Islamic philosophers like Ibn Arabi explain that God is an all-embracing, eternal reality. "Glory to Him who created all things, being Himself their very essence."

Even in Japanese Shintoism, a belief persists that a spiritual force imbues the material world with consciousness. Referred to as 'Tenchi Kane no Kami-Sama' or the spirit of the golden heavens and earth, this force is considered both a mindful and active presence within the universe, orchestrating all events and phenomena.

Finally, it's also worth noting that many indigenous belief systems across the Americas mention a universal energy force. For example, various North American First Nations hold a shared belief in a divine and unified spirit force that imbues all things (Solomon, 2015). This force is known by several names, such as the *Great Mystery, Sacred Other,* or *Great Spirit* (Means, 1993; Tinker, 2004). Similarly, in South America, ancient civilizations like the Aztecs embraced the concept of Teōtl, viewing it as an all-encompassing ultimate energy force. Teōtl, which signifies *sacredness* or *divinity,* is seen as omnipresent. Latin American scholar James Maffie explains Teōtl as "essentially power: continually active, actualized, and actualizing energy-in-motion... It is an ever-continuing process, like a flowing river... It continually and continuously generates and regenerates as well as permeates, encompasses, and shapes reality as part of an endless process. It creates the cosmos and all its contents *from within* itself as well as *out of* itself" (Maffie, 2014).

What is evident across these numerous and diverse examples is a consistent theme woven through civilizations, cultures, traditions, and faiths worldwide. Each of these distinctly different belief systems converges on a similar truth: there exists a universal energy force—a frequency that flows through the cosmos, permeating all entities and transcending both time and space.

This energy is known by many names and described in various ways, but the core idea remains consistent: everything is composed of energy, and this energy forms everything; it is a universal frequency mindset, if you will. When we draw connections between frequency and spiritual or philosophical doctrines, we begin to see a clearer picture. This isn't a grand conspiracy or hidden secret. Throughout human history, there have been those who recognized this force—this light, spirit, or cosmic energy—and used it not just to interpret reality, but to shape it. This cosmic energy exists within you. **YOU** have the power to harness and utilize it because **YOU** are composed of this same energy. It all comes down to tuning into the right frequency and finding the proper alignment.

MEDITATION & VISUALIZATION ACROSS SPIRITUAL TRADITIONS

When we label something as *sacred*, we're essentially recognizing it as possessing extraordinary worth or significance. This concept is closely linked to the practices of meditation and visualization. According to religious studies professor Sthaneshwar Timalsina, visualizing during meditation or prayer inherently adds value to the object or idea being focused on. He explains, "When we visualize something, we activate multiple cognitive mechanisms and the added meaning is gained through metonymic and metaphoric structures. The new value of an entity or the discovery of new meaning is often a consequence of the blend of the existing inputs." He further notes that in some spiritual traditions, particularly Hindu and Tantric ones, visualization is a technique used to deepen understanding of the mind's workings (Timalsina, 2017). This deeper understanding enables the blending of visualization with reality, thus influencing our daily lives. In your own efforts to manifest your goals and aspirations, viewing them as *sacred* can enhance their impact by elevating their significance in your mind.

In the previous section, we explored various faiths and spiritual traditions' perspectives on energy and frequency. Now, let's look into their views on the practice of visualization through meditation. Every spiritual tradition has developed its own unique meditative practices, which often incorporate symbols, narratives, and teachings specific to their culture.

First, let's define meditation. Meditation is a personal practice where an individual uses a technique—like focus, mindfulness, or visualization—to train their awareness and attention. The goal is to reach a state that is calm, stable, and clear, both cognitively and emotionally (Walsh, 2006; Goleman, 1988). These practices are most notably associated with Asian spiritual traditions such as Jainism, Buddhism, and Hinduism, but similar practices can be found world-wide (Dhavamony, 1982). The term 'meditation' comes from the Latin *meditatum*, meaning to think, contemplate, devise, or ponder. In the Catholic tradition, this term dates back to the 12th century and was used to translate the Sanskrit word *dhyana*, which means 'to contemplate' (Feuerstein, 2006). Given that *thinking*, *devising*, and *contemplating* all involve some form of visualization, it's clear why meditation and visualization are so closely linked. This connection is why I find it essential to explore their interactivity further.

Let's revisit Hinduism, where we find that meditation is a pivotal aspect of Indian spiritual life, notably embodied in the practice of yoga. Yoga comprises various *limbs*, each focusing on distinct objectives: intellectual study, devotion, religious performance, physical mastery, mind control, and the activation of subtle energies. Within Hindu practices, yoga and other forms of meditation often involve observance, posture, breath control, sense withdrawal, concentration, and contemplation, all contributing to a clear visualization of oneself and one's surroundings. The Brihadaranyaka Upanishad, an ancient Vedic text, illustrates this beautifully, stating, "having become calm and concentrated, one perceives the self (*ātman*) within oneself" (Flood, 1996). Thus, meditation serves as a tool for visualizing and understanding the self.

Similarly, in Jainism, meditation is considered a pathway to liberating the soul and realizing the self, aiming to attain pure consciousness beyond worldly attachments. This form of meditation involves clear contemplation, where practitioners visualize their conscious liberation from the binds of worldly attachments (Jansma, 2006). Like Hindu meditation, Jain meditation relies heavily on visualization, highlighting its critical role in achieving spiritual enlightenment and liberation.

For Buddhists, meditation is fundamentally about reaching nirvana, which represents a profound state of awakening. The term most akin to 'meditation' in original Buddhist languages is *bhāvanā*, translating as 'development'. Buddhism offers a rich tapestry of meditative practices, including over fifty methods for mindfulness and more than forty for concentration, leading to countless unique visualization techniques (Kamalashila, 2003). A key focus of Buddhist visualization is "maintaining the one [self] without wavering" (McRae, 1986). Through meditation, Buddhists aim to encourage deep personal growth, enhance insight, and gain a clear understanding of the nature of the phenomena around oneself, thereby overcoming life's obstacles and achieving spiritual liberation (Bodhi, 2005).

Taoism categorizes meditation into three primary forms: concentrative, insight, and visualization (Kohn, 2008). Taoist visualization involves envisioning lights and deities within the body, as well as solar and lunar essences, believed to promote health, longevity, and even immortality. These practices are integral to Chinese and Japanese martial arts and energy-focused exercises such as qigong, neigong, tai chi, and neidan, all considered forms of moving meditation. Practitioners of these disciplines focus on visualizing the flow and movement of energy (qi) within their bodies, a practice often termed *energetic visualization* (Perez-De-Albeniz, 2000).

In Jewish traditions, meditation has deep roots. The Torah, for example, mentions Isaac meditating in a field (Genesis 24:63), and the prophets in the Tanakh are described as meditators (Verman, 1977). One Hebrew word for meditation, *sîḥâ*, means to 'muse or rehearse in one's mind', highlighting its close relation to visualization (Kaplan, 1985). Early Jewish texts instruct believers to focus their minds on the Divine Presence and breathe with conscious gratitude (Genesis Rabba 14:9). Jewish mysticism, or Kabbalah, also uses visualization extensively, guiding followers to mentally explore spiritual realms in their meditative practices (Scholem, 1961).

In Christianity, meditation is considered a form of prayer that enables deliberate reflection on God's revelations (Zanzig, 1996). *Deliberate* is an important word there. The 12th century monk Guigo II developed Christian meditation practices based on earlier Benedictine traditions. Unlike Eastern meditations that might include chants or specific postures, Christian meditation involves a deeper introspection, often considered an advanced form of prayer. Saint Pio of Pietrelcina beautifully captured this, saying, "Through the study of books one seeks God; by meditation one finds Him" (Kelly, 2004). Many Christian theologians believe that through meditative prayer, an interior gaze can be refined, allowing the practitioner to hear an internal voice, the voice of God. Richard Foster suggests that meditation gives a person the *choice* to be transformed. Likewise, monastic writer Thomas Merton encouraged meditators to paint a scene in their imagination (Kelly, 2004). Pope Francis, in a 2021 General Assembly address, expanded on this by describing meditation as a journey towards understanding, involving thought, imagination, emotion, and desire. He stressed that the method of meditation should serve as a path towards spiritual and personal clarity, not the end goal itself. He noted, "This mobilization of faculties is necessary in order to deepen our convictions and in this way, only in this way, can we find ourselves" (Mayaki, 2021). This highlights how essential visualization is in Christian meditation, helping to deepen convictions and clarify personal and spiritual paths.

In Islam, meditation and visualization also hold significant roles, particularly demonstrated by the Prophet Muhammad's practices. He famously engaged in extended meditative retreats in the Cave of Hira near Mecca, where during one retreat, he received his first divine revelation from the angel Gabriel. Historical records show that Muslims, especially within Sufism, have developed specific meditation techniques that involve controlled breathing and the repetition of sacred phrases, aiming to reach deep concentration and introspective states (Dwivedi, 2016). The Quran and Hadiths highlight forms of meditation like *Fikr*, which means 'deep contemplation' in Arabic, and is highly valued; the Prophet Muhammad stated, "An hour of contemplation is of more value than seventy years of worship." Another significant practice is *tafakkur*, or 'reflection upon the universe', considered a vital act of worship that fosters emotional and cognitive growth by connecting with divine inspiration (Khalifa, 2001). Indeed, some Islamic sects believe that meditation reinvigorates *spiritual forces* (Effendi, 1973). While Islamic meditation may not explicitly involve visualization techniques, the act of *contemplation* inherently involves visualizing the subject of thought. Whether it's contemplating the self, the universe, or spiritual texts, visualization is subtly integrated into the meditative processes, facilitating deeper spiritual connections and personal transformation (Smith, 2000). This emphasis on contemplation is essential for spiritual growth within Islam, serving as a pathway to discovering and connecting with what might be described as universal energy.

I could explore additional faiths and belief systems, but the underlying message is clear: meditation inherently involves visualization to be effective. Across various traditions and cultures, meditation and visualization are intertwined methods for connecting with something greater than ourselves. This consistent recognition of their importance across diverse groups shows a universal appreciation for their roles in achieving a higher state of oneness with a greater power. This historical and widespread understanding underscores why incorporating meditation and visualization into our daily lives can significantly elevate our consciousness and help us realize our aspirations and intentions.

CULTIVATING INNER TRANSFORMATION THROUGH SPIRITUAL PRACTICE

Spiritual practice fundamentally aims to catalyze an inner awakening and transformation. As explored in this chapter, concepts of energy and frequency are deeply embedded within the spiritual frameworks of nearly every faith and religion, and these belief systems universally employ meditation and visualization to connect with universal energies or divine forces.

It's evident that many people seek some form of inner transformation or self-transformation, with meditation being a prevalent method across various demographics. According to a 2014 Pew Research Center poll, between 40% and 60% of Americans meditate at least once per week, depending on their religious affiliation. Interestingly, about 25% of atheists and agnostics also practice meditation regularly, indicating its widespread acceptance beyond religious contexts (Masci, 2018). Those who meditate regularly often report leading happier and *healthier* lives.

Supporting the benefits of meditation, visualization, and spirituality on both physical and cognitive health, Spanish researchers have suggested that incorporating a "body-mind-spirit model" into conventional healthcare could enhance patient outcomes by integrating focused spiritual practices like meditation (Montero-Marin, 2019). This approach is supported by research from Professor Cecelia Chan at the University of Hong Kong, which found that applying Eastern spiritual practices in clinical settings yielded positive results for patients with a range of health conditions, including cancer and mental health challenges (Chan, 2001, 2006).

We can confidently assert that the benefits of spiritual transformation manifest both mentally and physically. At the core of most inner transformation efforts is a strong desire to overcome various personal challenges, such as despair, loss, grief, anxiety, fear, failure, trauma, and deficiencies. Essentially, in our pursuit of self-transformation, we are deliberately shedding an older version of ourselves that was holding us back, allowing us to let go of existing *problems*.

Dr. Paul Leon Masters from the University of Sedona illuminates this by explaining that *problems* are merely "thought energies" originating in one's mind. "Whatever problems you have had, or are currently having, are a direct result of thought energies in your mind," he states. To transcend these problem energies, one must elevate to a higher frequency that aligns more closely with the universal energy (Masters, 2023). Masters advocates a theocentric approach where tapping into universal power effectively neutralizes problems. Consider meditation and visualization as tools—like antennae or receivers—designed to tap into these universal energy signals. By aligning with the right energy, you enable yourself to manifest at a higher level, supported by the power of the universe.

Some describe this *universal power* or *universal energy* as the 'God Frequency', a concept we've touched on earlier in this book. The God Frequency is rooted in ancient civilizations' understanding of the profound impact sound and frequency have on the human body and experience. Ancient Egyptian and Greek physicians used instruments to create specific frequencies believed to heal ailments such as mental disturbances, sleep deprivation, and digestive issues. Aristotle discussed how musical frequencies could evoke strong emotions and purify the soul. In the late 1800s, French physician Diogel documented the effects of live music on his patients, observing improvements in cardiac output, pulse rate, blood pressure, and respiratory rates, along with enhancements in the parasympathetic system (Meymandi, 2009).

While I won't expand further into the science here—as we've covered a great deal already—it's important to note that when we speak of the God Frequency, we are referring to how vibrations resonate with us on a deeply spiritual level. It's about how the frequencies of our minds, like the brainwaves discussed earlier, connect with broader, universal energy signatures. Inner transformation begins with this alignment of spiritual energy.

As we've seen in this discussion, meditation and visualization are key to aligning with higher consciousness and achieving inner transformation. Visualization, in particular, acts as a direct route to heightened awareness and spiritual awakening. It is fundamentally a creative process—what you envision can manifest in reality. Psychologist Michael Piechowski views inner transformation as a creative act, where developing oneself internally *creates* a new self (Piechowski, 2009). This view on transformation aligns with the broader concepts of manifestation and self-actualization. Philosopher Friedrich Nietzsche encouraged *self-recreation*, asserting that individuals who actively recreate themselves are the true artists of their own lives, epitomizing the essence of free spirits (Kaufman, 2015). To visualize is inherently to create; therefore, visualizing oneself amounts to creating oneself. When our spiritual selves are tuned to the necessary energies for this creative process, we ascend to a new spiritual level—mirroring the divine act of creation as when light was first visualized and then came into being.

Psychologist Hester McFarland Solomon describes self-transformation as *passage* from a two-dimensional to a three-dimensional self, illustrating the impact of spiritual alignment (Solomon, 2002). I believe it's possible to extend even beyond this, into a four-dimensional self, which we'll take a look at in a later chapter. For now, recognize that through meditation and visualization, by connecting with the universal energy, you transform two-dimensional ideas—your dreams, hopes, and desires—into tangible reality. Your words and thoughts, imbued with energy, have the power to effect change. **Change your frequency, change your destiny.**

At Qi Life, we deeply integrate the insights from spiritual traditions into the development of our technologies and devices. We understand the pivotal role that frequency plays in meditation and spiritual growth. Our frequency library includes a wide array of meditation and spirituality frequencies that surround you with the necessary vibrations to foster your spiritual awakening and speed up your journey toward holistic wellness. One standout offering is our Spiritual Awakening Collection, crafted to energize the mind and soul, transform personality traits, and deepen spiritual energy. This collection enhances your meditation experiences and boosts your spiritual awareness by leveraging ancient wisdom, as discussed throughout this chapter. It's just one of the many tailored solutions we provide, each designed to facilitate profound inner transformations and spiritual growth through your meditation and visualization practices.

In the upcoming chapter, I'll guide you through a meditation session, illustrating the powerful potential of this time-honoured practice and how it can help you attract the abundance you deserve in your life.

CHAPTER 8

MY GUIDED MEDITATION FOR RAPID MANIFESTATION

I n this chapter, I invite you to join me in a guided meditation—a peaceful interlude on your journey to inner transformation. Here, you can reflect on the insights gained from previous chapters and engage deeply with this newfound knowledge.

Before we embark on this meditative break, let's discuss *synergy* and its critical role in achieving comprehensive inner transformation. Originating from the Greek word 'synergia', meaning 'to work together,' synergy in contemporary terms is the interaction or cooperation of two or more entities to produce a combined effect greater than the sum of their separate effects. This concept is akin to *emergence*, where a whole exhibits properties its individual parts do not possess on their own.

Sociologist Lester Frank Ward referred to *social synergy* as "a form of cosmic synergy, the universal constructive principle of nature" (Ward, 1918). This idea is prevalent in philosophical and theological discussions. For instance, Christian theology introduces *synergism*, suggesting that salvation—or what some might call enlightenment—necessitates collaboration between the divine and the human, the earthly and the cosmic. Advocates for inner transformation often echo this sentiment, emphasizing the need for alignment with universal or cosmic frequencies. It's about achieving optimal energy flow, harmonizing internal and external elements so that our various components work together harmoniously, culminating in a self-actualized and transformed mind, body, and spirit.

The ancient practice of qigong, which continues to this day, exemplifies the synergistic and optimal flow of vibrational frequency that the Chinese have harnessed for millennia. Qigong combines synchronized movement, posture, breathing, and meditation to enhance spirituality, health, and physical prowess. Its core objective is to cultivate qi, the vital life force that is as essential as air for maintaining life balance (Plaugher, 2015; Cohen, 1999).

Scientific studies spanning decades have validated qigong's effectiveness in boosting both physical and mental health globally. Research has consistently linked qigong practice with significant health improvements in areas such as cardiovascular health, allergies, neuromuscular disorders, some cancers, hypertension, asthma, and the general aging process (Sancier, 1996). A 2010 report highlighted the "extraordinary experiences of Qi Gong practitioners on various levels of bio-psycho-spiritual/energetic functioning" (Posadzki, 2010). Moreover, a series of randomized controlled trials from 1993 to 2007 confirmed "consistent, significant results for a number of health benefits" associated with qigong (Jahnke, 2010). Qigong essentially manages the body's energy flow through what could be described as a biofeedback process, where the mind's influence over the body is profound. Intriguingly, this energy management appears to be transmissible between individuals. In various double-blind studies, both qi masters and their subjects displayed synchronized brainwave patterns when monitored with electroencephalograms (EEGs) (Machi, 1993). This suggests that synergy is not merely an internal phenomenon but can be a collective experience, enabling individuals to connect with one another's energy fields. This revelation underscores the incredible, almost superhuman capabilities of the human mind.

The power of the brain in this regard has inspired philosophers, thought-leaders, and meditation pioneers alike to build upon this sort of ancient wisdom: that the mind can regulate all. Among them was Texan electronics repairman José Silva, who in the 1940s began exploring psychology, psychic abilities, and brainwave activity. His research over the years culminated in the development of the Silva Method. Silva postulated that humans predominantly use their brains in a passive, beta wave state of consciousness. He argued that by slowing these waves to an alpha state, people could tap into higher cognitive functions, improve memory and learning, enhance intuition and creativity, deeper tranquility, and expedited healing (Swain, 2020).

Karin Barnes, a biomagnetic therapist and certified instructor of the Silva Method, elaborates on the course's approach: "The Silva Method involves guided exercises that teach you to enter a relaxed state. You then move on to mental techniques that harness visualization, imagination, positive thinking, and dynamic meditation. These exercises gradually expand your awareness and give you the control to influence your thoughts and mind. This enhanced control helps you address personal challenges, gain new perspectives, manifest your desires, and achieve happiness and success across various aspects of your life" (Barnes, accessed 2024).

Silva's teachings highlight that specific brain states can significantly boost awareness. In these states, the mind can project with precise intention, connecting with higher universal energies. This connection, according to Silva, enables individuals to receive guidance for self-actualization, solving problems and surmounting life's hurdles (Silva, 1977). Mindvalley founder Vishen Lakhiani speaks very highly of the

Silva Method, highlighting some of its key meditative benefits (Hope, 2023), including:

- Increased manifestation power
- Clear intuition
- Professional advancement
- Increased creativity
- Inner peace attainment
- Purpose development
- All-level healing
- Optimism maintenance

These benefits and more are a result of synergism between mind, body, and spirit, which Silva often referred to as the *ultramind*.

Dr. Joe Dispenza is a renowned thought leader and researcher who champions the impact of meditation in cultivating abundance, grounded in the principles of neuroscience and quantum physics. His work has illuminated for millions globally that our thoughts have the capability to shape our reality. For Dispenza, true abundance extends beyond mere material wealth; it encompasses the disciplined cultivation of a growth-oriented mindset, which in turn has the potential to rewire our brains. This shift in consciousness aims to align our thoughts, feelings, actions, and emotions with a frequency of abundance, thereby attracting our deepest desires into our lives.

Echoing Dispenza's sentiments, University of Oregon physics professor Amit Goswami speaks about "the power of quantum choice," emphasizing that our identity is not limited to the neural pathways currently formed in our brains. According to Goswami, our consciousness transcends these physical confines, offering us the freedom to explore new possibilities and access what Dispenza refers to as our 'ultramind'. In his book, *Evolve Your Brain*, Dispenza states, "We can all create a new life for ourselves and share it with others. We have the kind of hardware in our brain that allows us certain unique privileges. We can keep a dream or ideal in our mind for extended periods of time despite external environmental circumstances. We also have the capacity to rewire our brain, because we are capable of making a thought more real to us than anything else in the universe" (Dispenza, 2008). Meditation serves as a powerful gateway to unlocking the universe's vast potential, but achieving this requires us to move beyond the limitations traditionally imposed by society. Through meditation, we can explore and expand our consciousness, embracing the abundant possibilities that life offers.

With all that said, let's take a moment now to harmonize your energy flow. We're going to practice a simple, introductory meditation. Think of this as the first step toward emerging as a new, revitalized version of yourself. Your journey to inner transformation begins with a keen awareness of the present moment. In this session, we'll integrate the concepts of mindfulness, visualization, and energy flow that we've discussed throughout the book.

———

Before starting this meditation, find a peaceful, comfortable spot where you'll be undisturbed. You can sit or lie down, ensuring your spine remains straight. Rest your hands on your lap, palms facing up. Close your eyes and take several deep breaths to centre yourself. Ready? Let's begin.

STEP ONE: CENTRE

Stand or sit up straight, feet flat on the ground, and place your tongue against the roof of your mouth. Rest your hands one on top of the other on your navel.

Focus on your breathing. Inhale deeply through your nose, letting your abdomen expand as you fill your lungs with air. Exhale slowly through your mouth, imagining that you're releasing all your tension and stress with each breath.

As you exhale, hum the sound, "Hmmmmmm," and feel the vibration in your belly.

Repeat this process at least three times.

STEP TWO: ACTIVATE

Shift your focus to the energy inside your body. Imagine there's a radiant ball of light just below your navel. This light represents your life force, your energy. Picture it growing brighter and expanding with each breath.

Inhale deeply, and visualize this ball of light expanding, filling your entire body with vibrant, healing energy. As you exhale, vocalize a long "Haaaaaaaaaaw." Let go of any tension or negativity, imagining it dissolving into the air around you. Feel your energy field becoming more harmonious and balanced.

Continue this process for at least three times, or more if you feel the need.

STEP THREE: EXPAND

As you deepen your meditation, become fully present. Visualize the ball of light within you glowing more intensely. Gradually, let it expand, extending beyond the physical limits of your body to form a protective and comforting energy field around you, about three feet out.

Feel the warmth and safety of this energy, releasing any stress or negativity. Let this healing energy envelop you.

With each breath, imagine this field growing, filling the room with its luminous presence. Feel a connection to your surroundings, blending your energy with the collective consciousness around you. As you continue to breathe deeply, let the ball of light expand further, enveloping the entire Earth.

Sense the interconnectedness of all life as your energy reaches across the globe. Silently affirm: "I am energy, I am the creator of my reality." Let this mantra reinforce your connection to the universe and your power within it.

STEP FOUR: VISUALIZE

In this visualization, transport yourself into a future where your dreams and aspirations are already fulfilled. Imagine this future vividly, as if it is happening right now. See yourself living the success, healing, or abundance you've longed for. Picture every detail of this scenario as if it's a scene from your own personal movie of triumph.

Engage all your senses in this visualization. See the bright and vivid colours of your environment, hear the sounds that accompany your success, and feel the texture of the objects around you. Immerse yourself in the emotions and sensations of achievement and fulfillment.

Feel the joy and contentment that come from living in perfect alignment with your aspirations. Embrace the confidence that this future is not just a possibility, but within your reach. Let this experience bolster your belief in your ability to manifest this reality.

STEP FIVE: AMPLIFY

Allow yourself to fully absorb the emotions associated with achieving your dreams. Feel the rush of excitement, the sheer joy, and the profound sense of fulfillment coursing through you. Experience the deep gratitude for what you've accomplished, letting these feelings saturate every part of your being.

Let these powerful emotions build, intensifying within you, reaching a peak that fills you with energy. As this energy crescendos, feel it wash away any doubts or limitations you once had. Revel in this moment, basking in the radiant light of your realized potential.

Hold onto this feeling, knowing deeply that you are fully capable of manifesting your deepest desires and living a life rich with achievement and satisfaction. Embrace this truth and carry it with you, as a source of strength and inspiration.

STEP SIX: INTEGRATE

As you stay connected to these strong emotions, gently guide your attention back to the present moment and reconnect with your body. Feel the sensations in your body, the rhythm of your breathing, and your heart's steady beat. Allow the energy you've generated during this meditation to fill every cell, giving you renewed strength and purpose.

With each breath, ground yourself more deeply in the present, feeling stable and centred in your body. Remember, this powerful energy is always available to you, ready to support and inspire you to act on your dreams and goals right now. This energy is a constant ally, helping you to turn your deepest desires into reality.

STEP 7: CLOSING

As we conclude this meditation, imagine yourself as a leaf gently detaching from a tree, gracefully drifting from side to side, until it softly lands on the soil below. Embrace this peaceful feeling, a symbol of letting go and trusting the natural flow of life.

Gradually bring your focus back to your physical presence, noting the sensation of your breathing and the rise and fall of your belly. Relish the calm and tranquility that envelops you, aware that you've connected with a deep source of inner wisdom and strength.

When you're ready, slowly open your eyes, returning to the present with a refreshed sense of clarity and purpose. Recognize that by setting this powerful intention and starting the process of transformation, you've taken an important step towards realizing your dreams and shaping the life you desire.

―――――

How do you feel now? Reflect on your experience and *recognize the synergy* of mindfulness, visualization, and energy flow that has supported your personal transformation journey. By regularly engaging in this meditation, you can effectively harness these techniques to see positive changes emerge in your life.

To enhance and refine your practice further, explore the abundance and manifestation frequencies available through Qi Life. For instance, our Ultimate Abundance frequencies can significantly boost and automate your manifesting efforts. When combined with our Qi Coil™ devices, you can immerse yourself in potent frequencies that deepen your meditation and amplify the benefits for your physical, mental, and spiritual well-being. Continue your path to abundance and fulfillment by visiting QiLifeStore.com.

CHAPTER 9

THE SIXTH WAY TO LEARN

The cells in your body can communicate with one another, and like so much in the body, they do so through electromagnetic signal communication in order to share, adapt, and learn. Recall that every substance has its own unique energy signature—its own frequency... and the right frequency can trick your body into thinking it's being stimulated in a certain way. This fascinating biological capability is poised to spearhead the next scientific revolution, a movement that Qi Life is actively leading. We are exploring cellular communication technologies along two main paths: brain and body. For the brain, we focus on brainwave entrainment, while for the body, our research expands into areas like substance emulation and cellular information transmission.

In this chapter, I'll guide you through the groundbreaking frontier of cellular communication. This innovative science shows us how to teach our brain and body a *new way to learn* by syncing our cell activity with external signals. It's like having a sixth sense—besides hearing, seeing, touching, tasting, and smelling, you can also *learn* through frequencies. These frequencies help your cells adapt and change, opening up new possibilities for learning and health. We'll explore how this advanced technology can transform our understanding and improvement of human capabilities.

DECODING HOW CELLS COMMUNICATE

Cellular information transmission, or cell signalling, is vital for the small, constant tasks that cells in your body perform. These tasks include communicating with each other and reacting to changes in the environment. Essentially, each cell is programmed to send and receive specific signals, which help manage processes like immunity, tissue repair, and maintaining balance in the body, known as homeostasis. There are two types of cell communication: intercellular signalling, which is between cells, and intracellular signalling, which occurs within a cell itself (Mattaini, 2020).

Here's how it works: a cell picks up signals—these can be electromagnetic, electrochemical, or bioelectrical—from nearby cells or its surroundings. It then decodes this information and passes it on to other cells. This communication helps each cell adapt to constantly changing conditions (Sarkar, 2023). Recent research has shown that technology can directly control both the signals cells receive and how they respond. For example, light, which is a type of frequency, can be used to manage biochemical reactions in the cells (Valls, 2022). Other studies have shown that bioelectrical signals can guide communication between cells, influencing their behaviour to achieve specific results (Gerdes, 2013; Bukoreshtlliev, 2012). Cells can respond to a wide variety of environmental conditions, and interestingly, they can process multiple signals simultaneously. Cells use their complex communication networks to interact with each other, adjusting and refining their responses based on these interactions (Ullo, 2023).

The ability to influence cell communication with external stimuli has profound implications. It affects systems that control blood pressure, growth, menstrual cycles, digestion, red blood cell production, and glucose regulation, among others. When cell communication fails or is abnormal, it can lead to imbalances that cause diseases and adversely affect overall health (Reyes, 2023). Research shows that external frequencies can significantly impact dysregulation in various tissues, including the heart, brain, skeletal muscles, and intestines (Poelzing, 2021).

This demonstrates how external frequency stimulation can synchronize cellular functions and behaviours, promoting a desired biological balance.

SUBSTANCE EMULATION

When it comes to the body, one area where frequency regulation can have massive impact is in the realm of substance emulation. One crucial coenzyme involved in cell-to-cell communication is NAD (nicotinamide adenine dinucleotide) (Bogan, 2008; Billington, 2006). NAD is essential for proper cellular signalling and has been shown to play roles in addressing substance abuse, neurodegenerative diseases, aging processes, cancer protection, and more. It is even being explored for developing new antibiotic and antiviral medications, which are crucial as resistance to current treatments intensifies due to overuse and over-prescription (Bürkle, 2005; Navas, 2021; Lautrup, 2019; Yamboliev, 2009; Braidy, 2020; Fulleylove-Krause, 2020; Trapp, 2006; Li, 2017; Rizzi, 2002).

As discussed in my book *Life of Qi*, enzymes and neurotransmitters that facilitate cellular communication degrade over time, increasing disease likelihood as cells accumulate damage (Schultz, 2016). While healthy eating, regular exercise, and good sleep can mitigate this degradation, many people struggle to consistently meet these needs.

The challenge with vital biological substances like NAD is that they cannot directly enter cells; their production must be stimulated *internally*. This is why many turn to supplements, which can promote internal production. However, supplements—whether pills, powders, or injections—aren't suitable for everyone due to taste preferences, digestive issues, or reduced bioavailability based on individual health and body conditions.

Imagine if you could deliver the benefits of essential substances directly to every cell in your body—safely, naturally, and instantly. Well, it's possible, and it's done through what we call molecular frequency emulation, or substance emulation. This method uses sound and magnetic waves to replicate the effects of substances like NAD, leveraging the natural electromagnetic communication system of cells without the need to ingest the substances themselves.

By replicating the molecular and electromagnetic data of a substance's molecules, we can emulate their energy signature and effects, applying them directly to your cells. This process tricks cells into responding to these frequencies as they would to the chemical stimuli of the actual substances (Sternheimer, 1984, 1987; Benveniste, 1993). Substance emulation using frequency technology offers a revolutionary way to maintain, regulate, and enhance our physical and cognitive health by assisting natural cellular processes through electromagnetic methods, similar to brainwave entrainment which we'll explore next.

BRAINWAVE ENTRAINMENT

Much like cells in the body respond to external energy inputs, so too can the cells and tissues in your brain. Brainwave entrainment, which we touched on in Chapter Two, involves using external frequency stimuli to synchronize your brainwave state as desired. This technique programs specific frequencies with various oscillation and amplitude patterns, each tailored to induce different physical or cognitive outcomes. Your brain can lock onto these sound waves and synchronize with their rhythm, a process known as neural or brainwave entrainment. Essentially, your brain's large-scale electrical oscillations (your brainwaves) adjust to match the rhythm of the external sonic stimulus (Thaut, 2015).

A simple way to observe brain entrainment in action is to notice how you might tap your fingers or toes in time with music—that's your brainwaves aligning with the music's frequencies.

Recent scientific breakthroughs have shown that cellular behaviour in the brain can become synchronized (entrained) to external conditions. Studies have demonstrated that extracellular electric fields can trigger and regulate the collective rhythm of brain cells (Poelzing, 2021). This means external frequency inputs can condition your brain cells to operate in specific ways, essentially *training* your brainwaves to automatically adopt certain cognitive states.

Next, we'll explore the use of higher quantum frequencies in brainwave entrainment, examining how these advanced technologies can enhance cognitive functions and overall mental health.

ENTRAINMENT AND SYNCHRONICITY

Now that we've delved into cellular information transmission, substance emulation, and brainwave entrainment, we can see that these concepts are all interconnected by the principle of *entrainment* itself, also known as *synchronicity* or synergy. Recent advancements in entrainment technologies and therapies provide "precise spatial and temporal control of a cell's environment" (Jiménaz, 2022) and unlock oscillatory behaviours that are fundamental in biology. It's a well-known fact that cells constantly synchronize with one another, pointing to our ability to harness this biological phenomenon to redefine possibilities within the brain and body. This synchronization is fundamentally driven by oscillation, as all cells vibrate and possess a unique electromagnetic signature.

The influence of electrical fields, which are essentially oscillating wavelengths or *frequencies*, is well documented in affecting our bodies at both the molecular and cellular levels. This impact spans the neurons and circuitry in our brains to the tissues in our bodies, driven by the constant state of resonance in which every part of us exists.

Historical and modern research underscores the importance of this concept. From the early experiments by Fritsch and Hitzig in the 1870s that established the connectivity, excitability, and responsiveness of the brain (Fritsch, 1870; Hitzig, 1874), to contemporary studies on conditions like depression, epilepsy, and Parkinson's (Kringelbach, 2007), we continue to build upon the ancient understanding of energy fields, notably using soundwaves. This lineage of knowledge, enriched by thousands of years of observation, shows that extracellular energy field stimuli can prompt a wide range of responses across different cell types (Lee, 2023), revealing a complex and dynamic landscape of biological interaction influenced by frequency.

Psychologist Molly J. Henry of the Toronto Metropolitan University has conducted studies focusing on the complex rhythmic structures within our bodies and how they interact with rhythmic stimuli from the environment. Utilizing electroencephalography, one of her studies explored how the rhythms of our brains—specifically, neural oscillations—synchronize with synthetic sounds designed to mimic the wavelengths of speech and music. Henry and her team found that this neural synchronization is a constant, dynamic process. Their findings highlight how these synchronized frequencies can influence the brain's excitability across different bands, significantly impacting how effectively the brain processes environmental stimuli. This research reveals that our perception and interaction with the world, or our "psychophysical performance," can be profoundly affected by these external frequency bands (Henry, 2014).

HACK YOUR BRAIN FOR RAPID LEARNING AND TRANSFORMATION

At the start of this chapter, I introduced *resonant learning* as a revolutionary sixth method—a transformative way to learn. The key to unlocking this profound inner transformation is frequency, allowing us to tap into rapid biological learning processes that integrate the brain, body, and spirit. The means to this rapid and automated form of learning are developing fast across many scientific fields, but none more so than in the sound and light therapy spaces, both of which my team at Qi Life have been leading in. Sound therapy especially is pivotal for achieving the entrainment necessary to induce deep meditative states, which is foundational to our range of technologies and products.

Our devices, like the Qi Coil™ and Qi Coil Aura™, emit powerful, soothing qi energy (electromagnetic) waves that entrain your brain into relaxation and meditation. Through our webApp (members.Qi-Coil.com) or Resonant Console Tablet, you can select from an extensive range of proprietary quantum frequencies, each tailored to foster specific physical or cognitive outcomes. The main aim of this technology is to promote a deep relaxation response, facilitating a meditative state where homeostatic processes are activated, bringing your body into balance. More so, in such a state, your body's capacity to communicate—both sending and receiving signals—is enhanced, making it easier to connect with the subtle energies around you, Qi Coils™ are excellent tools for achieving synchronicity and aligning phase states, opening the door to higher states of consciousness and extraordinary capabilities.

Our users have experienced amazing physical and cognitive benefits using our Qi Coils™:

- Reduce anxiety and depression

- Increase feelings of relaxation and calmness
- Enhance your ability to adapt and cope with stress
- Relieve tension, headaches, insomnia, and pain
- Improve focus
- Better your memory and recall
- Increase energy and stamina
- Increase circulation for better cell function
- Elevate levels of oxygen throughout the body
- Speed up recovery times

These benefits—and more—can be significantly enhanced by using quantum and higher quantum frequencies as **audible** sound therapy while using Qi Coils™ for **silent** magnetic energy therapy at the same time (view advanced tutorials at QiCoil.com/setup). Our higher quantum frequencies are some of our most potent, scientifically proven to facilitate the deepest levels of meditation. Their unique properties will enable you to precisely tune your biofield. As I'll discuss in the next chapter, this precise tuning is key to unlocking even greater potential...

CHAPTER 10

QI COIL™ AND HIGHER QUANTUM FREQUENCY TECHNOLOGY

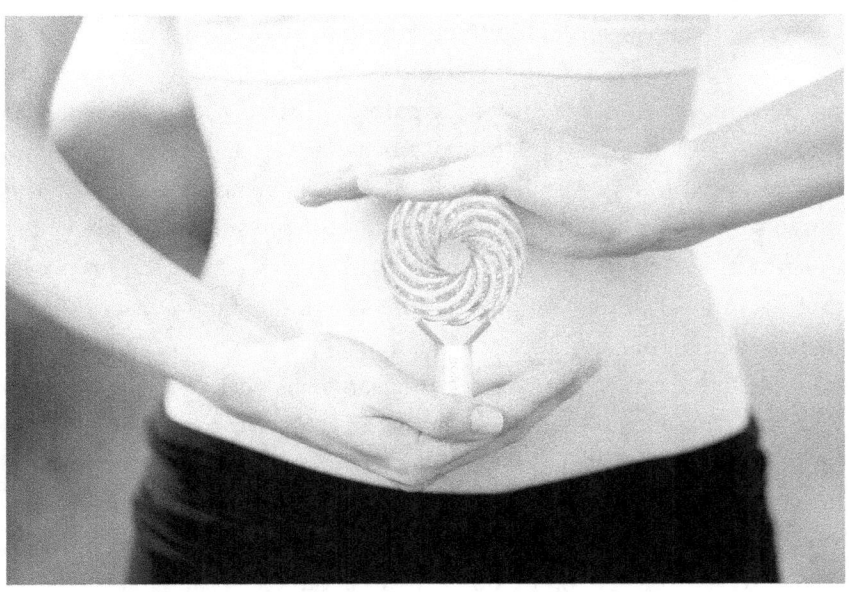

As we've explored through these pages, adopting a frequency mindset is crucial for your personal rapid transformation. The universe's resonant harmonics are ready for you to harness. Some of the most profound examples of this cosmic energy are found in higher quantum frequencies. I've reserved these for the final parts of the book because they truly encapsulate everything we've discussed. While these incredible wavelengths are complex, our technology at Qi Life simplifies their integration into your daily routine. We refer to this as *quantum resonance*, which forms the foundation for *rapid transformation* in your life—essentially a powerful bio-hack for unlocking true manifesting power. Truth be told, we've even gone beyond higher quantum frequencies, but I'll save that for the next chapter. For now, let's explore some quantum leaps in technology...

HIGHER QUANTUM FREQUENCIES

Quantum and higher quantum frequencies leverage our understanding of a *quantum universe*. Before diving into the specifics of these frequencies and their functionalities, it's beneficial to review some foundational concepts from quantum physics to provide historical context and clarify why these frequencies are incredibly potent.

Theoretical physicist John Archibald Wheeler once said, "We are not only observers. We are participators" (Brian, 2001). He believed that an interconnected, interdimensional, universal energy exchange was paramount to our understanding of consciousness and reality. The universe itself, he said, is *participatory*, and if physics is to answer the greatest questions we have about life and consciousness, he proposed that we must start demanding that physics understand existence itself (Brian, 2001). This sort of view was not new to Wheeler. Indeed, it's one that has been expressed for thousands of years. It was Buddha who said, "All that we are is the result of what we have thought. The mind is everything. What we think, we become." Wheeler simply built upon this ancient knowledge through the lens of quantum physics: "Spacetime tells matter how to move; matter tells spacetime how to curve" (Wheeler, 1998). In other words, our physical and material minds can exert energy that curves (or shapes) our reality.

Wheeler, alongside the renowned mathematical physicist Sir Roger Penrose, played a pivotal role in pioneering the advanced field of physics that posits consciousness as a byproduct of quantum mechanics. They proposed that the universe itself might possess a form of quantum consciousness (Taylor, 2010). Wheeler was a proponent of Hugh Everett's concept of the 'universal wavefunction', which describes the universe as existing in a universal phase state, also referred to as the *God Frequency* (Everett, 1957, 1973).

The concept that consciousness and reality are influenced by quantum physics has been supported by a host of respected researchers. For instance, physicist Alan Wolf, in his 1981 book *Taking the Quantum Leap*, explored the interplay between physics and consciousness. He demonstrated through simple experiments how our minds can shape different realities. Wolf noted that while a single thought only exists in the mind for a few milliseconds, focusing on it creates a 'train of thought'—a continuous series of similar thoughts. He explained, "If we maintain this focus, we are sending out the same wave function into the universe. The more we send this wave function into the universe, the more likely it is that this wave function will interact and cohere with a wave function similar to it. And the result will be a reality that we desire" (Taylor, 2010).

Many scientists describe this as the 'universal quantum connection', suggesting that we are quantumly connected to all things across time and space. This idea also resonates with ancient Hindu philosophy, where scriptures mention a cosmic database known as the 'Akashic Record'. This record purportedly contains a vibrational catalog of every event across the universe, encoded on distant matter—a universal imprint of time and space. According to tradition, this cosmic database is accessible to those who can tune into its vibrational frequencies, much like tuning into a specific radio station (Swanson, 2003). This concept aligns with Alan Wolf's proposal: by tuning our minds, we can interact with the frequencies that constitute the quantum universe.

So how exactly do we identify and qualify *higher quantum frequencies*? To understand how we can engage with these potent quantum energies, it's helpful to categorize different types of frequencies. Starting with single Rife frequencies, which operate in one dimension, we move to binaural beats that combine two frequencies, functioning in two dimensions. Quantum frequencies, which operate in three dimensions, bring us into more complex territory. The most advanced are the higher quantum frequencies, functioning in four dimensions with dynamic layers that allow for deep neural programming and effective brainwave entrainment. These higher quantum frequencies are particularly effective in enhancing health, well-being, and facilitating precise manifestations through their sophisticated resonance with the body's natural rhythms.

To understand different levels of frequencies, let's compare them to making music. Think of one-dimensional frequencies as playing just one note on a piano. It's simple and straightforward but not very exciting.

When we add a second dimension, it's like playing two notes at the same time. This sounds a bit better than just one note, but it's still pretty basic and doesn't really move you emotionally.

Moving up to three dimensions is like playing a chord, which is a group of notes that you play together. This starts to get more interesting because chords can make you feel different emotions; for example, a major chord might make you feel happy, while a minor chord could make you feel sad.

Finally, four-dimensional frequencies are like playing a whole song with many notes and chords following one after another. This is where things get really engaging because a song can change how you feel and carry you through a whole range of emotions. Just like a good tune can lift your spirits or calm you down, four-dimensional frequencies work in a similar way to reach deep into our feelings and can have a strong effect on our well-being.

To learn more about the science behind higher quantum frequencies, visit HigherQuantum.com.

Using the right frequency for your specific needs is crucial for achieving optimal results. While certain frequencies occur naturally, modern technology allows us to harness them in a more precise and controlled manner. Our Qi Life collection offers an unparalleled array of higher quantum frequencies, each meticulously refined and tested to cater to specific desires and outcomes. Unlike many in the field today who provide generic solutions, we at Qi Life are committed to identifying the exact sequence of higher quantum frequencies that best facilitate neural programming and targeted brainwave entrainment. This dedicated approach distinguishes us from competitors, enabling you to access these advanced technologies more swiftly and easily through direct frequency immersion. We refer to this cutting-edge application as Quantum Resonance Therapy.

HARNESSING FREQUENCY FOR WELLNESS: HOW QI COILS™ CAN HELP YOU THRIVE

The simplest way to engage in this form of therapy is through P.E.M.F., or pulsed electromagnetic field therapy. P.E.M.F. devices generate electromagnetic fields to stimulate specific physical and cognitive responses. Our Qi Coil™ devices, which I've discussed throughout this book, are prime examples of P.E.M.F. technology. Your body possesses its own electromagnetic field, known as the biofield or aura, which is continuously influenced by external frequencies—what we often refer to as 'electromagnetic pollution'. This exposure can affect your well-being because each cell in your body also produces its own electromagnetic field and communicates with other cells via electromagnetic frequencies. This exchange of electromagnetic energy keeps your body *in* or *out* of balance by controlling your body's chemical processes. When these processes are disrupted, it can lead to negative effects, but when they are positively influenced, the benefits can be significant, especially in manifesting your desires. Devices like our Qi Coils™ and Qi Coil Aura™ are designed to provide the precise frequencies to help synchronize and align your biofield with universal energies. Initially, my aim with these coil devices was to enhance our users' energy fields by 1% each day. However, with the introduction of higher quantum frequencies, we can now facilitate even more rapid transformations.

Qi Coils™ combine six Tesla-inspired technologies to promote wellness:

1. **High Dose P.E.M.F. Therapy** harnesses electromagnetic fields to enhance your overall well-being.
2. **Quantum Sound Therapy** employs soothing sound waves.
3. **Rife Frequency Therapy** targets specific health concerns using precise frequencies.

4. **Crystal Resonance Therapy** harnesses the natural power of crystals to boost the healing process.

5. **Scalar Energy Therapy** provides deep healing with scalar waves.

6. **EMF Protection Therapy** shields you from harmful electromagnetic fields, ensuring your safety.

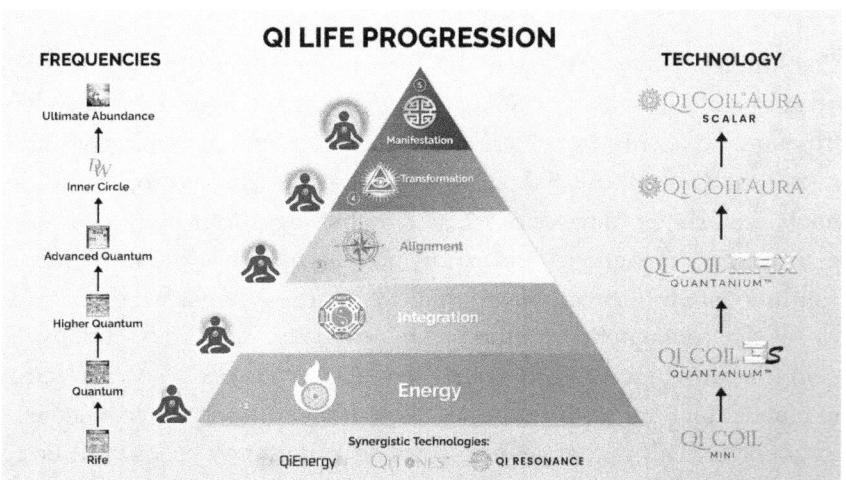

These coils offer a holistic approach to wellness, enhancing your physical, mental, and emotional health in a balanced way. They help create a serene and harmonious environment, reducing stress and anxiety, boosting energy, and enhancing mental clarity. The technology also supports detox and renewal processes, removing toxins and rejuvenating your body for renewed energy and vitality. Furthermore, Qi Coils™ are designed to strengthen the immune system and reduce inflammation, promoting better health.

The devices also encourage relaxation and tranquility, fostering inner peace through meditation and spiritual practices. They are effective in managing pain and improving joint mobility, which contributes to overall wellness. Additionally, the coils support gut health and nutrient absorption, ensuring a balanced and healthy digestive system.

THE SCIENCE BEHIND P.E.M.F. AND BRAINWAVE ENTRAINMENT

P.E.M.F. therapy finds its roots in magnetic field therapy, which has been utilized for its healing properties for thousands of years. Ancient healers from China, India, and Greece used naturally magnetized mineral magnetite, known as lodestones, to correct imbalances in the body's energy flow (Sivin, 1988, 1993; Zysk, 1993; Frawley, 2001; Emerson, 2019). Notably, Queen Elizabeth I's physician, Sir William Gilbert, widely regarded as the father of electrical science, employed magnets to alleviate the Queen's arthritis symptoms (Thompson, 1903). Historically, magnetic field therapy was applied for pain relief, reducing inflammation, enhancing sleep, treating infections, relieving stress, and improving blood circulation (Lawrence, 1998). Scientifically, this approach was rational because magnets produce a slight electrical current even without being electrically charged.

This practice later evolved into what we now know as electrotherapy—the medical use of electrical energy (IEEE, 1997). Early advocates like Giovanni Aldini, Luigi Galvani, Benjamin Franklin, and Nikola Tesla explored its benefits extensively. Electrotherapy has been used to ease chronic pain, and to treat mood disorders such as depression, insomnia, and anxiety, showing its wide-ranging potential in improving mental health (Hurley, 2008; Kroeling, 2013; Bronfort, 2004; Cantor, 2013).

P.E.M.F. therapy is a cultivated practice of longstanding ideas in both magnetic field theory and electrical field theory. Until the 19th century, scientists thought electricity and magnetism were separate, but then Einstein came into the picture, and we came to understand magnetism and electricity as different elements of the same unified field. This is what we call *electromagnetism*—the physical interaction that transpires between electrically charged particles (Ravaioli, 2010). After World War II, researchers in Russia began using pulsed electromagnetic fields extensively, finding it beneficial for a wide range of medical conditions from heart disease to cancer and even mental health issues (Jerabeck, 1998).

As the Cold War progressed, P.E.M.F. devices started to be used more broadly. One of the earliest was the Helmholtz coil, designed by Hermann von Helmholtz. It produced a near-uniform magnetic field that was designed to surround and envelop a patient. Much like early computers, Helmholtz coils were massive instruments, but such devices quickly became smaller as the technology further developed. The most well-known variations resemble thick yoga mats, with flat coil systems embedded into them, controlled by frequency generators. These mats are still popular today, but I always thought they were too large and disrupted daily life because they required users to lie down, taking up space and pausing their activities.

This challenge inspired my team and me to push the boundaries further, aiming to make P.E.M.F. therapy more practical and accessible. We envisioned creating devices that were small enough to carry around and versatile enough to be used in various everyday situations —whether standing, sitting, or moving. This adaptability offers significant benefits, especially when integrating this therapy with approaches like brainwave entrainment and neural programming. With portability and flexibility comes tremendous advantage, particularly when taking this form of therapy into the brainwave entrainment or neural programming side of things. As we explored P.E.M.F.'s applications in quantum resonance therapies, we knew we had a game-changer on our hands. Much like the general history behind P.E.M.F. therapy, quantum applications also have a fascinating scientific history behind them.

In 1927, physicist Paul Dirac published *The Quantum Theory of the Emission and Absorption of Radiation*, in which he proposed the novel idea that even the vacuum of space is not completely empty but filled with a background of oscillating electromagnetic fields known as zero-point energy. This field manifests as 'quantum fluctuations', which are temporary changes in energy at any point in space. This phenomenon is believed to enable 'resonance fluorescence', where atoms in different energy states can interact with these quantum electromagnetic fields, leading to what is known as *superposition*—where these energy states synchronize (Weisskopf, 1981). Dirac's theory laid the early scientific groundwork for the concept of a coherent, synchronized quantum state, which would later be referred to as 'quantum consciousness'.

Quantum consciousness is the ability to tap into universal knowledge (universal frequencies). Think of all the mass and energy in the universe as a computer: cosmic hardware. Universal knowledge is the cosmic software that governs the system. Philosopher Ervin Laszlo views this cosmic data as a frequency connection between all things. He suggests that this interconnectivity reduces down even to the individual being. He calls this 'whole-system coherence'. Every aspect of our bodies is in continuous and instant communication. This "makes reliance on biochemistry alone insufficient," he says. "Quasi-instant, nonlinear, heterogeneous, and multi-dimensional correlations" among all our cells, organs, and systems suggest that our bodies are macroscopic quantum systems, driven by the same resonant frequency (Laszlo, 2004).

Recall from Chapter One when we discussed Winfried Otto Schumann's 1950s discovery of the Schumann resonances—these global electromagnetic resonances are within the same range as human brainwaves and impact all of us, establishing a kind of global energy network that can organize and influence human consciousness. It's suggested that these resonances play a crucial role in electromagnetic synchronization that may be essential for human intelligence (Cherry, 2003). This means they're part of the underlying structure that connects us all at a quantum level.

These resonances not only influence human health and mental well-being but also affect phenomena beyond our senses and even extend their influence to non-human life. For example, they can trigger biochemical changes in trees and plants that signal the transition between seasons (NASA, 2013). Researcher Lewis Hainsworth speculated that human evolution itself might be synchronized with Schumann resonances, suggesting that our brainwave patterns developed in response to these atmospheric signals. This could explain why disruptions in these resonances are linked to significant health issues, including immune system anomalies, disrupted sleep patterns, changes in blood pressure and hormone levels, and neurological disturbances (Cherry, 2002; Miller, 2003). This clear connection found right here on Earth illustrates how deeply frequencies can influence life at both microscopic and macroscopic levels.

At the microscopic level, brainwave entrainment unlocks extraordinary possibilities. Your brain is a network of billions of neurons that communicate through synapses, enabling every thought, action, and emotion you experience. Each neuron, like every cell in your body, responds to resonant frequencies.

Neurons can synchronize with external frequencies and rhythms, effectively learning or relearning innate responses. As C. Maxwell Cade, a physicist and meditation expert, once explained, this represents "a new way of learning, a way of relearning, or realizing for the first time, what the body already knows—how to act, how to feel, even how to heal—if we listen" (Cade, 1979).

Your neural networks provide feedback to your brain's limbic system, generating the chemical effects we know as emotions and feelings (Morgane, 2005). By intentionally influencing these neural pathways, you can modify how your body expresses emotions and even alter your genetic responses through new neural programming. Throughout history, energy masters and healers have achieved this through deep meditative and healing practices. However, not everyone has the time to master these techniques. This is where engaging with the right frequencies can make a significant difference, allowing you to align your body's chemical responses with your mental intentions more efficiently.

Furthermore, your limbic system acts as the control centre for your autonomic nervous system, which oversees essential body functions like hormone secretion, temperature, breathing, blood sugar, and heart rate—processes your body manages automatically (Blessing, 1997). These systems adjust based on how you emotionally react to your experiences. By aligning your neural activities through entrainment to foster desired emotional responses, you can also encourage your body to adopt healthier autonomic outcomes. Imagine your brain and body operating in seamless harmony, achieving a new level of consciousness —a quantum state. As discussed in my book *Life of Qi*, these new habits become ingrained in your cerebellum, becoming part of your intrinsic behaviour. Think about it: meditative states becoming instinctive, increased productivity becoming second nature, and overcoming psychological traumas without lingering effects. Envision your body initiating its own healing processes, efficiently managing stress, fighting diseases with enhanced vigour, and promoting brain health as you age. These capabilities and more are not just fantastical—they're the new superhuman abilities enabled by neural programming and quantum resonance therapy.

ANCIENT WISDOM FOR MODERN SOLUTIONS

If we accept that the universe and everything within it operates on quantum energy, then it follows that these energies can be tuned, entrained, transmitted, and received. This concept is the foundation of achieving quantum consciousness. Neural programming and brainwave entrainment through P.E.M.F. represent the pinnacle of millennia of wisdom and scientific progress, offering solutions for today *and* visions for tomorrow.

By utilizing quantum resonance as a tool for self-development, personal evolution, and growth, you can begin to engage new thoughts, actions, and emotions. Consequently, your body's biological systems can also develop and evolve. Research at Heinrich Heine University has shown how synchronizing neuronal activity through external stimuli can serve as a mechanism for extensive inter-neuronal communication, impacting the entire body (Schnitzler, 2005). I want you to remember that *whole approach*—the holistic approach. Consider your body, mind, and spirit as a single instrument that, when finely tuned, reveals its full potential. This *quantum potential* is what drives me each morning and has led me to personally oversee the development of our higher quantum frequencies. This advanced form of resonance therapy is my greatest passion. Higher quantum frequency immersion allows you to receive direct neuronal download through mathematically tuned harmonics rooted in quantum numerical expressions such as Fibonacci ratios, phi, pi, sacred geometry, and zero-point energy. I aim for you to achieve a profound spiritual connection, heightened psychic abilities, enhanced manifestation power, sharp mental clarity, increased vitality, deep tranquility, and vibrant joy—key aspects to fine-tuning your physical, cognitive, emotional, and spiritual health through neural programming. This is the wonder of energy therapy, and at Qi Life, we have developed devices tailored to every need.

I firmly believe that to change your destiny, you simply need to change your frequency. By aligning yourself with the universe's energy, profound transformations are possible. My conviction stems not only from the daring scientific explorations of some of the brightest minds and the spiritual practices of history's most enlightened energy masters but also from countless firsthand testimonials from individuals who have used my devices and resources. This technology, I am convinced, will define the evolution of humanity in the decades to come. It represents a new scientific revolution—an adventurous new realm of healing, rehabilitation, and development for the mind, body, and spirit.

In our next and final chapter, I'll summarize the core insights from this book and share my vision for a prosperous future for us all. I will also unveil the next step in quantum technology as promised earlier—a breakthrough I believe will fast-track your journey to ultimate abundance and prosperity.

CHAPTER 11

YOUR DESTINY AWAITS: UNLOCKING YOUR HIDDEN DRAGON AND ULTIMATE ABUNDANCE

You've reached the final chapter of our journey together. Through these pages, I hope you've discovered transformative insights that resonate deeply, revealing new truths and awakening your potential to master your own destiny. At the heart of everything we've explored is a simple, powerful truth: it all revolves around frequency. **Change your frequency, change your destiny**.

To embark on a significant inner transformation and unlock your manifesting powers, you must first embrace a frequency mindset—a growth mindset, a *quantum mindset*. Viewing the world through this lens enables you to achieve the ultimate abundance and automated prosperity neural programming we've been aiming for since the beginning. You'll be ready to unleash your hidden potential, but let's first reflect and envision...

Quantum physics shows us that the constant motion and vibration of every cell and molecule in your body produces *resonance*. I invite you to see this resonance as a roadmap for your life's journey. By understanding it as a blueprint for possible futures, you begin to comprehend the imbalances, dysregulations, and desynchronizations blocking your path. Regardless of whether you're starting from a challenging place or you're already on stable ground but facing unseen barriers, you can harness your body's resonant frequencies to adjust your personal energy field. This equilibrium of health and wellness will be your springboard to success. What's more, when your body, mind, and spirit are in harmony, you can influence the harmony around you. Your energy can positively affect others, enhancing your own balance in return. This concept is rooted in what we've discussed as the Law of Attraction, but it's also known scientifically as *coherence*: a synchronized order of matter and electromagnetic fields. This harmony is not just a personal gain; it's a shared, expansive benefit that enriches everyone and everything around you.

This concept forms the cornerstone of emerging fields like quantum electrodynamics and quantum biology—the cutting-edge frontiers of science. As outlined by electrical engineer Antonio Manzalini and internal medicine specialist Bruno Galeazzi, every part of our bodies—from cells to tissues to organs—operates with its own specific wave functions. These functions are synchronized in a perfectly orchestrated multi-level coherence (Manzalini, 2019). Many researchers, like physicist Menas Kafatos, argue that the existence of the biofield challenges traditional reductionist approaches and suggests that our understanding of resonant frequencies in relation to biology can lead to an integrated understanding of consciousness and the living universe (Kafatos, 2015).

I refer to this as our *quantum tomorrow*, a future where we collectively elevate our resonance to bring our frequencies into greater harmony and balance. By achieving this, we can foster a global consciousness and, from there, cultivate global abundance. But this monumental change begins with *YOU*, on an individual and personal level. By raising your own frequency, you contribute to this global shift, helping to shape a future where unity and collective prosperity are within our grasp.

ABUNDANT YOU, ABUNDANT WORLD: CULTIVATING PERSONAL GROWTH FOR GLOBAL IMPACT

Leadership expert Dov Baron emphasizes the impact of our resonances on our relationships and ultimately on global consciousness. He suggests that our interpersonal connections—whether at home, work, or in society—play a crucial role in shaping our collective energy. Baron explains that our beliefs and resonances not only mold our leadership qualities but also define our lives. "What we resonate, we attract as relationship, and what we attract as relationship determines what we resonate," he notes (Baron, 2018).

This concept of interconnectedness is echoed in the work of researchers Tam Hunt and Jonathan Schooler from the University of California. They explore the notion of coherence—achieving an energy balance and a unified frequency that fosters community and collective well-being. Hunt and Schooler refer to this pursuit as "*the easy part of the hard problem,*" which is central to their resonance theory of consciousness (Hunt, 2019).

In 2019, their research looked into how synchronization and harmonization of vibrations and frequencies relate to neural consciousness. They address the 'hard problem', or the 'combination problem', which challenges us to understand how micro-conscious entities, like individual human beings, combine to form a higher-level, macro-consciousness. Essentially, they seek to determine how individual consciousness and resonance can merge to elevate a collective consciousness and resonance, enhancing our understanding of ourselves and our universe.

In his influential book *Sync: How Order Emerges from Chaos in the*

Universe, Nature, and Daily Life, mathematician Steven Strogatz captures the essence of universal order, saying, "At the heart of the universe is a steady, insistent beat: the sound of cycles in sync... These feats of synchrony occur spontaneously, almost as if nature has an eerie yearning for order" (Strogatz, 2003). This observation ties back to the ancient insights of philosophers and spiritual leaders who have long understood the universe's fundamental language—energy.

The universe consistently signals a desire for harmony and synchronization, urging us to align our vibrations not only metaphorically but also literally. This concept of achieving a 'shared resonance' allows us to experience the benefits of a collective harmony. As neuroscientist Pascal Fries has posited, this phenomenon can be understood as 'communication through coherence'. Similarly, researchers Hunt and Schooler, who developed the 'General Resonance Theory of Consciousness', argue that through shared resonance, humans can enhance their collective consciousness. They describe this interconnected state of consciousness as *panexperientialism,* suggesting that "Biologically evolved entities rely on resonance [a shared vibratory frequency] between their constituent parts to achieve far more complex types of consciousness" (Hunt, 2019).

This principle is further supported by quantum and biological physics, which teach us that everything in the universe is in perpetual oscillation. An especially fascinating aspect of this universal principle is the phenomenon of harmonic oscillation, where two entities vibrating at different frequencies can, when they come close together, begin to oscillate synchronously, enhancing the speed and richness of information and energy flows (Strogatz, 2003).

Biologist Walter Freeman's work has shown that certain processes occur so quickly that they must be driven by electrical field signalling. He describes how "spatial patterns... or carrier waves repeatedly re-synchronize" over vast distances, supporting the notion that rapid communication across the brain involves more than just chemical signals (Freeman, 2006). This finding lends credibility to ancient philosophies, which posited that all matter, at some level, shares a form of consciousness. Biophysicist Christof Koch further explains that consciousness is intrinsic to organized matter. "As far as chemistry and biology are concerned, charge is an intrinsic property of these particles. Electrical charge does not emerge from non-charged matter—it is inherent. Similarly, consciousness is embedded in the organization of the system," he states (Koch, 2014). Koch emphasizes that the resonance patterns of individuals can synchronize information flows, enabling the emergence of a larger, harmonized entity (Koch, 2004). "The type of interconnection and combination between resonating structures is key for consciousness to expand," adds researcher Tam Hunt (Hunt, 2019).

The emerging field of quantum biology challenges the long-standing skepticism within academic biology about the relevance of quantum phenomena to biological systems. Research now confirms that quantum processes are not only possible but prevalent within biological systems, playing a crucial role in the rapid transfer of energy both within and outside our bodies (Lambert, 2013; Weingarten, 2016). This understanding of *quantum resonance*—our ability to both receive and emit energy through quantum mechanisms—underscores the potential of a *quantum tomorrow*.

That's precisely why we at Qi Life have strategically focused on developing higher quantum frequencies. We view quantum dynamics as the key to unlocking rapid, intentional inner transformation, enabling greater manifestation and, consequently, greater abundance. Through this enhanced abundance, individuals can reach new heights of consciousness and self-awareness. However, personal abundance is not our sole objective. As we've discussed, our broader aim is to transform this personal abundance into global abundance. By achieving a harmonized resonance within oneself, you not only improve your own life but also enhance the potential for those around you to resonate with and benefit from this energy.

HEALING THE WORLD TOGETHER

To bridge the gap between personal abundance and broader, global solutions, it starts by spreading the word and raising awareness about the power of scientifically proven phenomena. The more people who understand the reality of their personal energy fields, the more good they can do in the world.

Many advocates of resonance are working hard on fast-tracking this process. One organization's work has certified more than sixteen-hundred energy healing practitioners through intense two-year training programs. These practitioners have subsequently worked with hundreds of thousands of people around the world, addressing physical and cognitive imbalances with responsive energy approaches (Eden, 2020). Such efforts are crucial for expanding global resonance potential and represent a significant opportunity for the future—an *energy-informed* population could spark remarkable innovations in healthcare and foster the interconnected resonance needed to strengthen interpersonal relationships at community and international levels.

This approach could fundamentally change how we address global challenges like climate change, war, and disease, making the science of frequency a cornerstone of an integrative approach to solving civilization's major problems.

Hindu philosophy describes human history in terms of four *yugas*, or ages, that represent cycles of creation and destruction. Currently, we are believed to be living in the Kali Yuga, an era characterized by conflict, aggression, and moral decline (Smith, 2009). However, it is said that this will eventually give way to the Satya Yuga, an age of truth, righteousness, and spiritual enlightenment, where harmony and order (*dharma*) will be restored (Kane, 1936).

Our ability to manifest our own individual abundance can usher us into this type of new era. Our personal quantum energy can extend its influence like ripples across humanity. These frequencies can help synchronize others to a similar state, producing a communal resonance that can open new possibilities. When we share this frequency and resonate together, we tap into what Hunt and Schooler describe as *panexperientialism*, a shared global consciousness (Hunt, 2019). This collective state could not only inspire but practically enable us to solve the world's significant challenges—not merely through intention but through a profound energetic alignment that extends from individual to collective, connecting all of humanity with the universe.

This vision of a unified future is what I call our *quantum tomorrow*, where changing our frequency can fundamentally change our destiny.

My life's work is dedicated to the harmonizing process of continual inner transformation, aiming to unlock the full potential of a resonant life. This journey starts by helping others, like you, to quickly and easily transform themselves. That's why all our products, including the Qi Coil™ and our higher quantum frequencies, are designed to integrate effortlessly into your daily life. I encourage you to elevate your perception of what a fulfilling life looks like, to seek higher states of consciousness, and to deepen your understanding of existence. By aligning your resonant frequency, you open the door to abundance and activate the manifesting powers innate within you.

Taking this vision further, we are advancing beyond even our higher quantum frequencies with our latest initiative—the Hidden Dragon Club. Aimed at those who wish to escape the confines of an unfulfilled life, this exclusive new frequency collection offers transformative prosperity programming. The Hidden Dragon Club's Abundance Ultimate package features ELEVEN powerful quantum meditation and abundance frequencies, each tuned to key aspects of prosperity from wealth to love, creating an ideal environment for you to automatically manifest wealth and prosperity.

Discover the transformative power of our revolutionary collection. Each frequency in the Ultimate Abundance exclusive collection is crafted to synchronize your energy with the universal frequencies of abundance. Whether you're aiming for financial success, personal fulfillment, or deeper, more meaningful relationships, Ultimate Abundance offers you the key to a life brimming with prosperity and joy. Unlock your potential and embrace a future where your aspirations align seamlessly with the abundant energy of the universe. Allow me to introduce you to this collection. The frequencies included are:

1. **Universal Abundance:** feel a profound connection with the universe, experiencing a sense of awe and wonder as you tap into the endless possibilities and opportunities that *your* life has to offer.
2. **Joyful, Fulfilled and Grateful:** embrace a heart full of joy and a mind filled with gratitude, leading to an enriched and deeply satisfying life where *your* every day feels more meaningful and rewarding.
3. **Instantaneous Luck:** enjoy a delightful sense of serendipity and fortune, feeling as though the universe is conspiring to bring *you* good luck and positive outcomes at every turn.
4. **Abundance Achieved:** experience the exhilaration and fulfillment of seeing *your* dreams and goals materialize, bringing a sense of accomplishment and pride in *your* achievements.
5. **Business Success:** feel empowered and confident as *your* business endeavours flourish, bringing a sense of achievement and recognition in *your* professional life.
6. **Financial Wealth:** experience the peace and security that comes from financial stability and abundance, freeing *you* from stress and anxiety about *your* future.
7. **Prosperity Attained:** relish in the joy and contentment of a prosperous life, enjoying the luxury, comfort, and freedom that comes *your* way with true abundance.
8. **Attract Soul Mate:** feel the deep emotional connection and

joy of attracting *your* soul mate, experiencing love, companionship, and a profound sense of belonging.

9. **Grounding and Programming:** experience a sense of clarity and focus, feeling grounded and steadfast in *your* pursuit of goals, with a mind programmed for success and fulfillment.

10. **[Coil] Abundance Ultimate 1:** (optimized for Qi Coils™) Amplify the power of abundance frequencies, enhancing *your* overall experience.

11. **[Coil] Abundance Ultimate 2:** (optimized for Qi Coils™) Further intensify the resonance with abundance, solidifying *your* journey towards prosperity.

As a member of the Hidden Dragon Club, you'll unleash your inner dragon, which is about automating the three essential steps to manifestation: visualize, resonate, amplify.

Embracing your inner dragon involves tapping into all the incredible benefits of Abundance Ultimate—a set of advantages we've detailed throughout this book:

- **Effortless and Time-Efficient:** easily integrate these frequencies into your daily routine without the need for active engagement or an extensive time commitment.
- **Science Backed:** Abundance Ultimate frequencies are grounded in the principles of bioenergetics and sound therapy, offering a modern and researched-based method for personal growth.
- **Targeted and Personalized:** each frequency is specifically designed for different aspects of abundance, providing a more tailored approach than generic self-help solutions.
- **Non-Invasive and Safe:** Abundance Ultimate is a comfortable and risk-free option, with no known side effects, compared to more intrusive methods.
- **Cost-Effective:** unlike so many other offerings on the market, Abundance Ultimate is a one-time investment that offers enduring value, particularly in contrast with the ongoing costs of workshops or personal coaching sessions.

- **Holistic:** this collection covers a wide range of life's aspects, from financial wealth to personal fulfillment, supporting your overall well-being.
- **Convenient and Accessible:** you can enjoy these transformative frequencies from the comfort of your home, saving time and avoiding the hassle of travel.
- **Coil Device Compatible:** the Abundance Ultimate collection can be enhanced by our advanced coil devices like Qi Coil™ and Aura Coil™, for improved effectiveness.

The transformative power of Qi Coils™ in attracting abundance has been vividly illustrated through a series of compelling stories from users who have experienced significant changes in their lives, some of which we've touched on before. Here's a reminder of those, and a closer look at a few others, showcasing how Qi Coils™ have helped individuals manifest abundance in various forms:

Jerome shared his story of overcoming daunting financial challenges through the Qi Coil™. Faced with over $3 million in debt, he found solace and solutions in the frequencies offered by the Qi Coil™. Not only did he manage to devise a strategy to significantly reduce his debts, but he also attracted new financial opportunities that seemed perfectly aligned with his needs.

Kelly, an IT company owner, shared how incorporating the Qi Coil's™ luck frequency into his daily routine led to immediate success. The very next day, his company secured two high-value deals, nearing a million dollars in total new revenue. This sudden windfall highlighted the Qi Coil's™ ability to enhance business outcomes almost instantaneously.

Dr. Joe Vitale experienced the magnetic effect of Qi Coils™ soon after his interview with me. Intrigued by a frequency designed for attracting ultimate abundance, he tried it and was astounded when he received an unexpected $32,000 cheque the very next day. This moment of serendipity reaffirmed his belief in Qi Coils'™ ability to manifest financial blessings.

Sarah, a luxury real estate agent from New Jersey, was initially skeptical about the Qi Coil™. However, her perspective shifted dramatically when, within just three hours of using a frequency aimed at financial success, she earned a $90,000 commission. This was quickly followed by another deal that netted her an additional $20,000, showcasing the Qi Coil's™ potent impact on her professional prosperity.

Steve, a real estate investor found that Qi Coil™ frequencies had a surprising and welcome effect on their business dealings. This individual received a call from a potential client who was not referred by anyone but seemed to have been attracted by the frequencies' influence. This new connection led to a significant financial transaction, further proving the Qi Coil's™ efficacy in drawing prosperity.

Lastly, Devora, who had long aspired to work with certain influential figures found that after using the Qi Coil™, these desires began to materialize. People who had been mere names on a vision board for years suddenly became accessible, offering new opportunities for collaboration and growth. This story underscores the Qi Coil's™ ability to not only attract financial wealth but also to forge valuable connections that can lead to long-term success and fulfillment.

No more missed opportunities for wealth. No more continued financial struggles. No more stagnation in your personal growth. No more lost or strained connections. No more persistent negative mindsets. Break free of it all by adopting the ultimate frequency mindset: the ultimate abundance mindset... in The Hidden Dragon Club.

Your destiny, and the destiny of humanity awaits. I'm privileged and motivated each and every day to help you manifest the abundance of a resonant life, and I hope you've been inspired in these pages to receive the cosmic energy that has surrounded you since the day you were born. It's all around you. It's yours for the taking. Harness it. Share it. Be well and do good with it.

———

I extend my personal invitation to join our Hidden Dragon Club so you can discover your own Hidden Dragon. Amplify your strengths and overcome obstacles.

Visit HiddenDragonMastery.com

EXPLORE MORE RESOURCES

CONTINUE YOUR LEARNING JOURNEY

Review This Book on Amazon: Help others by sharing your thoughts. Your feedback is invaluable. Visit **FrequencyReview.com**

Book a Free Product Consultation: Tailor your transformational journey with expert guidance. Visit **QiLifeAdvisor.com**

ENHANCE YOUR PRACTICE

Free 30-Day Qi Gong Challenge: Elevate your daily practices with guided exercises. Visit **DavidWongQiGong.com**

Abundance Workshop: Master wealth manifesting techniques in our interactive workshop. Visit **FrequencyDestiny.com**

DISCOVER FREQUENCY TECHNOLOGIES

Qi Coil™ Rife & P.E.M.F. Therapy: Discover the transformative benefits of Qi Coil™ therapy. Visit **QiLifeStore.com**

AUTOMATED QUANTUM HEALING & ABUNDANCE

Programming: Experience a 7-Day Free Trial of automated programming for wellness and prosperity. Visit **QiEnergy.Ai**

Free Quantum Frequencies: Access transformative frequencies at no cost. Visit **Members.QiCoil.com**

Abundance Frequencies: Begin attracting abundance with higher quantum frequencies. Visit **QiLifeStore.com/pages/abundance**

Ultimate Abundance Frequencies: Harness our most potent frequencies for wealth and prosperity. Visit **HiddenDragonClub.com**

Change Your Frequency.
Change Your Destiny.

REFERENCES

Acharya, S., et al.(2012) Mirror neurons: Enigma of the metaphysical modular brain. Journal of Natural Science, Biology and Medicine, 3(2).

Adams, T. (2015, February 8). Interview – Norman Doidge: the man teaching us to change our minds. The Observer, Neuroscience, from: https://www.theguardian.com/science/2015/feb/08/norman-doidge-brain-healing-neuroplasticity-interview

Aftanas, L.I., Golocheikine, S.A. (2001, September 7). Human anterior and frontal midline theta and lower alpha reflect emotionally positive state and internalized attention: high-resolution EEG investigation of meditation. Neuroscience Letters, 310(1).

Alexander, M.L., et al. (2019, March). Double-blind, randomized pilot clinical trial targeting alpha oscillations with transcranial alternating current stimulation (TACS) for the treatment of major depressive disorder (MDD). Translational Psychiatry, 9(106).

Alexander, R. (2020, February). The neuroscience of positive emotions and affect: Implications for cultivating happiness and wellbeing. Neuroscience & Biobehavioural Reviews, 121.

Ariel, D.S. (2006). Kabballah: The Mystic Quest in Judaism. Lanham, MD: Rowman & Littlefield.

Arts, T., ed. (2014). Oxford Arabic Dictionary. Oxford: Oxford University Press.

Ashby, F. G., et al. (1999). A neuropsychological theory of positive affect and its influence on cognition. Psychology Review, 106.

Bacconier, S., et al. (2002, August). New crystal in the pineal gland : characterization and potential role in electromechano-transduction. Conference papers, URSI General Assembly.

Barak, Y. (2006, October 6). The immune system and happiness. Autoimmunity Reviews, 5(8).

Barnes, K. (accessed 2024). The Silva Method Syllabus. From: https://www.karinbarnes.co.uk/the-silva-method-syllabus

Baron, D. (2018, April 9). Relationships for Raising Global Consciousness. Medium, from: https://medium.com/thrive-global/relationships-for-raising-global-consciousness-8b981727b351

Behan, C. (2020, December). The benefits of meditation and mindfulness practices during times of crisis such as COVID-19. Irish Journal of Psychological Medicine, 37(4).

Benveniste, J. (1993). Transfer of Biological Activity by Electromagnetic Fields. Frontier Perspectives, 3(2).

Beres, D. (2020, November 26). Why is DMT Called The Spirit Molecule?. Psychedelic Spotlight, from: https://psychedelicspotlight.com/why-is-dmt-called-the-spirit-molecule/

Billington, R.A., et al. (2006). Emerging Functions of Extracellular Pyridine Nucleotides. Mol. Med., 12(11–12).

Black, D.S., Slavich, G.M. (2016, January 21). Mindfulness mediation and the immune system: a systematic review of randomized controlled trials. Annals of the New York Academy of Sciences, 1373(1).

Blascovich, J., Katkin, E. (1993) Cardiovascular reactivity to psycho logical stress and disease. American Psychological Association; Washington, DC.

Blessing, W.W. (1997). Inadequate Frameworks for Understanding Bodily Homeostasis. Trends in Neurosciences, 20(6).

Blumenthal, J.A. (1985). Relaxation therapy, biofeedback, and behavioral medicine. Psychotherapy: Research, Practice, Training, 22.

Bodhi, B. (2005). In the Buddha's Words: An Anthology of Discourses from the Pali Canon. Simon and Schuster.

Bogan, K.L., et al. (2008). Nicotinic Acid, Nicotinamide, and Nicotinamide Riboside: A Molecular Evaluation of NAD+ Precursor Vitamins in Human Nutrition. Annual Review of Nutrition, 28.

Braden, G. (2008). The spontaneous healing of belief. Carlsbad, CA: Hay House.

Braidy, N., et al. (2020). Sobriety and Satiety: Is NAD+ the Answer?. Antioxidants, 9(5).

Brian, D. (2001). The Voice of Genius: Conversations with Nobel Scientists and Other Luminaries. Basic Books.

Brod, S., et al. (2014, May 21). 'As above, so below' examining the interplay between emotion and the immune system. Immunology, 143.

Bronfort, G., et al. (2004). "Non-Invasive Physical Treatments for Chronic/Recurrent Headache. The Cochrane Database of Systematic Reviews, 3.

Bukoreshtliev, N.V., et al. (2012, December 8). Mechanical cues in cellular signalling and communication. Cell and Tissue Research, 352.

Bürkle, A. (2005). Poly(ADP-ribose). The Most Elaborate Metabolite of NAD+. FEBS J., 272 (18).

Cade, C.M., & Coxhead, N. (1979). The Awakened Mind: Biofeedback and the Development of Higher States of Awareness. Wildwood House Limited.

Cantor, D.S., & Evans, J.R. (2013). Clinical Neurotherapy: Application of Techniques for Treatment. Academic Press.

Chalovich, J.M. (2012). Franklinization: Early Therapeutic Use of Static Electricity. ScholarShip, East Carolina University.

Chan, C., et al. (2001). A body-mind-spirit model in health: an Eastern approach. Social Work in Health Care, 34.

Chan, C., et al. (2006, July). East meets West: applying Eastern spirituality in clinical practice. Journal of Clinical Nursing, 15(7).

Cherry, N.J. (2002). Schumann Resonances, a Plausible Biophysical Mechanism for the Human Health Effects of Solar/Geomagnetic Activity. Natural Hazards, 26(3).

Cherry, N.J. (2003). Human Intelligence: The Brain, An Electromagnetic System Synchronized by the Schumann Resonance Signal. Medical Hypotheses, 60(60).

Chopra, D. (2004) Unlocking the hidden dimensions of your Life. New York, NY: Three Rivers Press.

Choudhry, O., Gupta, G., Prestigiacomo, C.J. (July 2011). On the surgery of the seat of the soul: the pineal gland and the history of its surgical approaches. Neurosurgery Clinics of North America, 22(3): vii.

Coate, H.H.J. (1966, December). The Rai and the Third Eye North-West Australian Beliefs. Oceania, 37(2).

Cohen, K.S. (1999). The Way of Qigong: The Art and Science of Chinese Energy Healing. Random House of Canada.

Culp, J. (2013). Panentheism. Stanford Encyclopedia of Philosophy.

D'Acquisto, F. (2017, March) Affective immunology: where emotions and the immune response converge. Dialogues in Clinical Neuroscience, 19(1).

Dadashi, M., Birashk, B., Taremian, F., Asgarnejad, A.A., Momtazi, S. (2015, January). Effects of Increae in Amplitude of Occipital Alpha & Theta Brain Waves on Global Functioning Level of Patients with GAD. Basic Clinical Neuroscience, 6(1).

Davidson, R., et al. (2003). Alterations in brain and immune function produced by mindfulness meditation. Psychosomatic Medicine, 65(4).

Davidson, R., Begley, S. (2012). The Emotional Life of Your Brain. Avery.

Descartes, R. (2002). "The Passions of the Soul". In Chalmers D (ed.). Philosophy of the Mind. New York: Oxford University Press, Inc.

Dhavamony, M. (1982). Classical Hinduism. Università Gregoriana Editrice.

Dhillon, N., Singh, A.D., Dua, H.S. (February 1, 2009). "Lord Shiva's third eye". British Journal of Ophthalmology. 93(2).

Dispenza, J. (2008). Evolve Your Brain: The Science of Changing Your Mind. Health Communications Inc.

Dispenza, J. (2019). Becoming Supernatural: How Common People are Doing the Uncommon. Hay House, Inc.

Doidge, N. (2016). The Brain's Way of Healing. Penguin Life.

Dweck, C.S. (2006). Mindset: The New Psychology of Success. Ballantine Books.

Dwivedi, K.N. (2016). Book Reviews. Group Analysis, 22(4).

Edelman, G. (1987). Neural Darwinism: The Theory of Neuronal Group Selection. New York, New York: Basic Books.

Eden, D., & Feinstein, D. (2020). Development of a Healthcare Approach Focusing on Subtle Energies: The Case of Eden Energy Medicine. Advanced Mind Body Medicine, Summer, 34(3).

Edlow, B.L., et al. (2012, June). Neuroanatomic connectivity of the human ascending arousal system critical to consciousness and its disorders. Journal of Neuropathology and Experimental Neurology, 71(6).

Effendi, S. (1973). Directives from The Guardian. Hawaii Bahá'í Publishing Trust.

Emerson, D.W. (2014). The Lodestone, from Plato to Kircher. Preview, 2014(173).

Emory, M. (2019, August 21). The Creative Science Behind The Emotional Brain: A Q&A with Dr. Richard J. Davidson.BrainWorld, from: https://brainworldmagazine.com/the-creative-science-behind-the-emotional-brain-a-qa-with-dr-richard-j-davidson/

Espel, E.S., et al. (2016, August 30). Meditation and vacation effects have an impact on disease-associated molecular phenotypes. Translational Psychiatry, 6, e880.

Everett, H. (1957). Relative State Formulation of Quantum Mechanics. Reviews of Modern Physics, 29(3).

Everett, H., et al. (1973) The Many-Worlds Interpretation of Quantum Mechanics, Princeton Series in Physics. Princeton University Press.

Feuerstein, G. (2006). Yoga and Meditation (Dhyana). Moksha Journal, 1.

Flood, G. (1996). An Introduction to Hinduism. Cambridge: Cambridge University Press.

Foster, J.J., et al. (2017). Alpha-Band Oscillations Enable Spatially and Temporally Resolved Tracking of Covert Spatial Attention. Psychological Science, 28(7).

Frawley, D., & Ranade, S. (2001). Ayurveda, Nature's Medicine. Lotus Press.

Fredrickson, B.L., Levenson, R.W. (1998) Positive emotions speed recovery from the cardiovascular sequelae of negative emotions. Cognition and Emotion, 12.

Fredrickson, B.L. (2000, October). Positive emotions as strengths: Implications for the VIA taxonomy. In: Vaillant GA Chair, editor. Toward the VIA taxonomy of strengths and virtues. Symposium cosponsored by the Values in Action Institute and the Positive Psychology Network; Fogelsville, PA.

Fredrickson, B.L. (2001, June 24). The Role of Positive Emotions in Positive Psychology. American Psychology, 56(3).

Freeman, W. J., and Vitiello, G. (2006). Nonlinear brain dynamics and many-body field dynamics. Electromagnetic Biology and Medicine, 24.

Fries, P. (2005). A Mechanism for Cognitive Dynamics: Neuronal Communication Through Neuronal Coherence. Trends in Cognitive Sciences, 9(10).

Fritsch G. (1870). Uber die elektrische Erregbarkeit des Grosshirns. Archiv für Anatomie, Physiologie und Wissenschaftliche Medicin, 37.

Fulleylov-Krause, B.K., et al. (2020). Nicotinamide Mononucleotide Treatment Increases NAD+ Levels in an iPSC Model of Parkinson's Disease. bioRxiv (online pre-print), Retrieved March, 2022, from: https://www.biorxiv.org/content/10.1101/2020.05.06.080911v1

Garland, E., et al. (2010). Upward spirals of positive emotions counter downward spirals of negativity: Insights from the broaden-and-build theory and affective neuroscience on the treatment of emotion dysfunctions and deficits in psychopathology. Clinical Psychology Review, 1(16).

Gerdes, H.H. (2013, February 26). Cell-to-cell communication: current views and future perspectives. Cell and Tissue Research, 352.

Gilbert. C.D., Li, W., Piech, V. (2009). Perceptual learning and adult cortical plasticity. The Journal of Physiology. 587(12).

Goleman, D. (1988). The meditative mind: The varieties of meditative experience. New York, NY: Tarcher.

Goleman, D. (1995). Emotional intelligence. New York: Bantam Books.

Gordon, A. (2015, January 23). Author who brought neuroplasticity to the masses has new book on the brain's power to heal. Toronto Star, from: https://www.thestar.com/life/author-who-brought-

neuroplasticity-to-the-masses-has-new-book-on-the-brain-s-power/
article_004820bb-fa82-5ed2-a5ab-a91a53c33105.html

Grob, C.S. (2002). Hallucinogens: A Reader. TarcherPerigee.

Hebb, D.O. (1949). The Organization of Behavior. New York, NY: J.
Wiley.

Henry, M.J., et al. (2014, October 14). Entrained neural oscillations in
multiple frequency bands comodulate behavior. Proceedings of the
National Academy of Sciences, 111(41).

Herrmann, N. (1997, December 22). What is the function of the various
brainwaves? Scientific American. https://www.scientificamerican.
com/article/what-is-the-function-of-t-1997-12-22/

Hicks, E., Hicks, J. (2004). Ask and It Is Given: Learning to Manifest
Your Desires. Carlsbad, CA: Hay House Inc.

Hicks, E., Hicks, J. (2006). The law of attraction. Carlsbad, CA: Hay
House Inc.

Hitzig E. (1874). Untersuchungen über das Gehirn: Abhandlungen
physiologischen und pathologischen Inhalts (A. Hirschwald).

Holler, F., et al. (2007). Principles of Instrumental Analysis (6th
Edition). Cengage Learning.

Hope. (2023). Silva Method Review (2023): Is The Ultramind System
Legit? Center for Worklife, from: https://centerforworklife.com/gen/
personal-development/silva-method/?utm_campaign=20988601132&
utm_source=x&utm_medium=cpc&utm_content=&utm_term=&
seg_aprod=&ad_id=&gad_source=1&gclid=CjwKCAjwzN-
vBhAkEiwAYiO7oLUmPI1U6B051I0MDiHhg5MMrsszNQqI23_fbCeSi
DvxQN_jEhLplBoCUqEQAvD_BwE

Hurley, M.V., et al. (2008). Non-Exercise Physical Therapies for Musculoskeletal Conditions. Best Practice & Research: Clinical Rheumatology, 22(3).

Hunt, T., et al. (2019, October 31). The Easy part of the Hard Problem: A Resonance Theory of Consciousness. Frontiers in Human Neuroscience, 13.

IEEE (Institute of Electrical and Electronics Engineers). (1997). The IEEE Standard Dictionary of Electrical and Electronics Terms (6th ed).

Jafari, S. (2020, Summer). A comparative study of the Eye of the Heart in Islamic Sufism and the Third Eye in Yoga. Journal of Literary Arts, 12(2), No. 31.

Jaffe, E. (2007, May 1). Mirror Neurons: How We Reflect on Behaviour. Association for Psychological Science, from: https://www.psychologicalscience.org/observer/mirror-neurons-how-we-reflect-on-behavior

Jahnke, R., et al. (2010). A Comprehensive Review of Health Benefits of Qigong and Tai Chi. American Journal of Health Promotion, 24(6).

Jamal, A. (2002) The One-Minute Sufi: Timeless and Placeless Principles in Small Doses. Azim Jamal Publications.

Jang, S.H., Kwon, Y.H. (2020, October 14). The relationship between consciousness and the ascending reticular activating system in patients with traumatic brain injury. BMC Neurol, 20.

Jansma, R., et al. (2006). Yoga and Meditation. Introduction to Jainism. Prakrit Bharti Academy.

Jefferson, R.B. (1982). The Doctrine of the Elixir. Coombe Springs Press.

Jerabeck, J., & Pawluk, W. (1998). Magnetic therapy in eastern Europe: A Review of 30 Years of Research. W. Pawluk.

Jiménaz, A., et al. (2022, June 6). Principles, mechanisms and functions of entrainment in biological oscillators. Interface Focus, 12(3).

Kafatos, M.C., et. al. (2015). Biofield Science: Current Physics Perspectives. Global Advances in Health and Medicine, 4.

Kamalashila. (2003). Meditation: The Buddhist art of tranquility and insight. Birmingham: Windhorse Publications.

Kane, P. V. (1936, September). "Kalivarjya (actions forbidden in the Kali Age)". Journal of the Bombay Branch of the Royal Asiatic Society. 12(1-2).

Kaplan, A. (1985). Jewish Meditation: A Practical Guide. New York: Schocken Books.

Kasmer, J. (2023, July 15). Traditions and religions teach about energy as Spirit. Times Colonist, from: https://www.timescolonist.com/blogs/spiritually-speaking/traditions-and-religions-teach-about-energy-as-spirit-7281257#:~:text=Panentheism%20says%20that%20-God%2C%20Divine,is%20both%20transcendent%20and%20immanent.

Kaufman, S.B. (2015, December 28). How Creativity Makes Us Feel Alive. Medium, from: https://medium.com/@sbkaufman/how-creativity-makes-us-feel-alive-13923fff3a30#:~:text=According%20to%20Michael%20Piechowski%2C%20the,literally%20creating%20a%20new%20self.

Kaushik, M., Jain, A., Parvez, S. (2020, September 28). Role of Yoga and Meditation as Complimentary Therapeutic Regime for Stress-Related Neuropsychiatric Disorders: Utilization of Brain Waves Activity as Novel Tool. Journal of Evidence-Based Integrative Medicine, 25.

Keating, T. (2012). The Thomas Keating Reader: Selected Writings from the Contemplative Outreach Newsletter. Lantern Books.

Kelly, E. (2004). The Rosary: A Path Into Prayer. Loyola Press.

Khalifa, R. (2001). Quran: The Final Testament. Universal Unity.

Kingsland, J. (2019). Am I Dreaming?: The Science of Altered States from Psychedelics to Virtual Reality and Beyond. Atlantic Books.

Koch, C. (2004). The Quest for Consciousness: A Neurobiological Approach. Boston, MA: Roberts Publishers.

Koch, C. (2014, January 1). Is Consciousness Universal? Scientific American, from: https://www.scientificamerican.com/article/is-consciousness-universal/

Kohn, L. (2008). "Meditation and visualization". The Encyclopedia of Taoism.

Kringelbach M.L., et al. (2007). Translational principles of deep brain stimulation. National Review of Neuroscience. 8.

Kroeling, P., Et. al. (2013). Electrotherapy for neck pain. The Cochrane Database of Systematic Reviews, 8.

Lagopoulos, J., et al. (2009, November 18). The Journal of Alternative and Complementary Medicine, 15(11).

Lambert, N., et al. (2013). Quantum biology. Nature Physics, 9.

Lang, S.B., et al. (1996, August 16). Piezoelectricity in the human pineal gland. Bioelectrochemistry and Bioenergetics, 41.

Laszlo, E. (2004). Science and the Akashic Field: An Integral Theory of Everything. Inner Traditions.

Lautrup, S. (2019). NAD+ in Brain Aging and Neurodegenerative Disorders. Cell Metabolism, 30(4).

Lawrence, R., & Rosch, P. (1998). Magnet Therapy Book: The Pain Cure Alternative. Prima Publication.

Lazar, S.W., et al. (2005). Meditation experience is associated with increased cortical thickness. NeuroReport, 16(17).

LeDoux, J. (1992). Emotion and the limbic system concept. Concepts in Neuroscience, 2.

Lee, S.Y., et al. (2023, February 15). Cell class-specific electric field entrainment of neural activity. bioRxiv, version 4.

Li, J., et. al. (2017). A Conserved NAD Binding Pocket that Regulates Protein-Protein Interactions During Aging. Science, 355(6331).

Liu, H., M.D., & Perry, P. (1997). Mastering Miracles. Warner Books.

Lokhorst, G.J. (2015). Descartes and the Pineal Gland. Stanford: The Stanford Encyclopedia of Philosophy.

Loonis, R.F., Brincat, S.L., Antzoulatos, E.G., Miller, E.K. (2017, October 11). A Meta-Analysis Suggests Different Neural Correlates for Implicit and Explicit Learning. Neuron, 96(2).

Losier, M.J. (2006). Law of attraction. New York, NY: Wellness Central.

Lustenburger, C., Boyle, M.R., Foulser, A.A., Mellin, J.M., Frölich, F. (2015, June). Functional role in frontal alpha oscillations in creativity. Cortex, 67.

Machi, Y. (1993). Various measurements of qigong masters for analyzing qigong mechanism. Society for Mind-Body Science, 2(1).

Maffie, J. (2014). "Teotl". Aztec Philosophy, Understanding a World in Motion. University Press of Colorado.

Manzalini, A., & Galeazzi, B. (2019). Explaining Homeopathy with Quantum Electrodynamics. Homeopathy.

Markowsky, G. Britannica online. Physiology, from: https://www.britannica.com/science/information-theory/Physiology

Martindale, C., Hasenfus, N. (1978, April). EEG differences as a function of creativity, stage of the creative process, and effort to be original. Biological Psychology, 6(3).

Masci, D., et al. (2018, January 2). Meditation is common across many religious groups in the U.S.. Pew Research Center, from: https://www.pewresearch.org/short-reads/2018/01/02/meditation-is-common-across-many-religious-groups-in-the-u-s/

Masters, P.L. (2023, April 30). Universal Power Over Problems. The Theocentric Way of Life, Volume 5: Module 51.

Masunaga, S. (2017, April 21). A Quick Guide to Elon Musk's New Brain-Implant Company, Neuralink. Los Angeles Times. Retrieved March, 2022, from: https://www.latimes.com/business/technology/la-fi-tn-elon-musk-neuralink-20170421-htmlstory.html

Mattaini, K.R. (2020). Introduction to Molecular and Cell Biology. Roger Williams University Press.

Mayaki, B. (2021, April 28). Pope at Audience: Meditating is a way of encountering Jesus. Vatican News, from: https://www.vaticannews.va/en/pope/news/2021-04/pope-francis-general-audience-meditation-prayer.html

McGreevey, S. (2011, January 21). Eight weeks to a better brain: Mediation study shows changes associated with awareness, stress. The

Harvard Gazette, from: https://news.harvard.edu/gazette/story/2011/01/eight-weeks-to-a-better-brain/#:~:text="Although%20the%20practice%20of%20meditation,the%20MGH%20Psychiatric%20Neuroimaging%20Research

McRae, J. (1986). The Northern School and the Formation of Early Ch'an Buddhism. University of Hawaii Press.

Means, R. (1993). Where White Men Fear To Tread. Macmillan.

Medeiros, J. (2017, October 4). How to 'game your brain': the benefits of neuroplasticity. Wired UK, from: https://www.wired.co.uk/article/game-your-brain

Meinhardt, J., Pekrun, R. (2003). Attentional resource allocation to emotional events: an ERP study. Cognitive Emotion, 17.

Merritt, R. (1999). Chill out: it does the heart good, from: http://dukemednews.org/news/article.php?id=353

Merzenich, M.M., Jenkins W. M. (1993). Cortical representation of learned behaviors, in Memory Concepts, ed. Andersen P. (Amsterdam, NL: Elsevier).

Merzenich, M.M., de Charms, C. (1996). Neural representations, experience and change, in The Mind-Brain Continuum, eds. Llinas R., Churchland P. (Boston, MA: MIT Press).

Merzenich M.M. (2001). Cortical plasticity contributing to child development, in Mechanisms in Cognitive Development, eds McClelland, J., Siegler, R. (Mahwah, NJ: Ehrlbaum).

Merzenich, M.M. (2013). Soft-Wired: How the New Science of Brain Plasticity Can Change Your Life. San Francisco: Parnassus Publishing.

Merzenich, M.M., et al. (2014). Neural plasticity-based rehabilitation. Trends in Neurosciences, 37(6).

Meymandi, A. (2009, September). Music, Medicine, Healing and the Genome Project. Psychiatry, 6(9).

Miller, R.A., & Miller, I. (2003). Schumann's Resonances and Human Psychobiology, O.A.K.

Miller, R.J. (2014). Drugged: The Science and Culture Behind Psychotropic Drugs. Oxford University Press.

Miller, R.J. (2017). Psychedelic Medicine: The Healing Powers of LSD, MDMA, Psilocybin, and Ayahuasca. Park Street Press.

Montero-Marin, J., et al. (2019, March 27). Religiosity and Meditation Practice: Exploring Their Explanatory Power on Psychological Adjustment. Frontiers in Psychology, 10(630).

Montiel, I., et al. (2005). Biophysical Device for The Treatment of Neurodegenerative Diseases. In A. Méndez-Vilas (ed.). (2003, October 13-18). Recent Advances in Multidisciplinary Applied Physics. [Conference presentation]. First International Meeting on Applied Physics (APHYS-2003), Badajoz, Spain.

Morgane, P.J., et al. (2005). A Review of Systems and Networks of the Limbic Forebrain/Limbic Midbrain. Progress in Neurobiology, 75(2).

Mullins, E. (2008, August). The Process of the Law of Attraction and the 3rd Law, Law of Allowing. University of Wisconsin-Stout Thesis Paper, from: http://www2.uwstout.edu/content/lib/thesis/2008/2008mullinse.pdf

Nakamura S., Sakaguchi T. (1990). Development and plasticity of the locus coeruleus: a review of recent physiological and pharmaceutical experimentation. Progress in Neurobiology, 34.

NASA (National Aeronautics and Space Administration). (2013, May 28). Schumann Resonance. J. Wilson, Ed. Retrieved May, 2022, from: https://www.nasa.gov/mission_pages/sunearth/news/gallery/schumann-resonance.html

Navas, L.E., et al. (2021). NAD+ Metabolism, Stemness, the Immune Response, and Cancer. Signal Transduction and Targeted Therapy, 6(2).

Nelson, K. (2007). The law of attraction, from: http://www.abundance-and-happiness.com/law-of-attraction.html

Nidup, J., et al. (2017, November 7). Improving Well-Being in Bhutan: A Pursuit of Happiness or Poverty Reduction?. Social Indicators Research, 140.

Nigal, S.G. (2009). Vedic Philosophy of Values. New Delhi: Northern Book Centre.

Ostir, G.V., et al. (2000) Emotional well-being predicts subsequent functional independence and survival. Journal of the American Geriatrics Society, 48.

Pagés Ruiz, F. (2001). Krishnamacharya's Legacy. Yoga Journal, May/June Ed.

Parrish, S. (2015, March 2). Carol Dweck: A Summary of Growth and Fixed Mindsets. Farnam Street, from: https://fs.blog/carol-dweck-mindset/

Paul, K., ed. (1987). T'ai Chi Ch'uan and Meditation by Da Liu. Routledge.

Pearce, K. (2022, October 1). Understanding Brain Waves: Beta, Alpha, Theta, Delta + Gamma. DIYGENIUS. https://www.diygenius.com/the-5-types-of-brain-waves/

Perez-De-Albeniz, A. (2000). Meditation: Concepts, Effects And Uses In Therapy. International Journal of Psychotherapy, 5(1).

Piechowski, M. (2009, November 2). Is inner transformation a creative process? Creativity Research Journal, 6(1-2).

Pillay, S. (2011, November 17). Is There Scientific Evidence for the "Law of Attraction"?. HuffPost, from: https://www.huffpost.com/entry/is-there-scientific-evide_b_175189

Plaugher, N. (2015). Standing Qigong for health and martial arts. Zhan Zhuang: Ebooks Corporation.

Poelzing, S., et al. (2021, December 7). Initiation and entrainment of multicellular automaticity via diffusion limited extracellular domains. Biophysics Journal, 120(23).

Posadzki, P. (2010). The Psychology of Qi Gong: A Qualitative Study. Complementary Health Practice Review: Journal of Evidence-Based Integrative Medicine, 15(2).

Radler, B. (2012). The Emotional Life of Your Brain, by Richard J. Davidson, a review. Wisconsin Academy of Sciences, Arts & Letters, from: https://www.wisconsinacademy.org/magazine/emotional-life-your-brain-how-its-unique-patterns-affect-way-you-think-feel-and-live%25E2%2580%2594and-ho

Rahal, D., et al. (2023, July). Positive and negative emotion are associated with generalized transcriptional activation in immune cells. Psychoneuroendocrinology, 153.

Ratey, J. (2001) A User's Guide to the Brain. New York: Vintage Books.

Ravaioli, F.T., Et. al. (2010). Fundamentals of Applied Electromagnetics (6th ed.). Prentice Hall.

Ray, A. (2021, December 1). Reticular Activating System for Manifestation and Visualization, from: https://amitray.com/reticular-activating-system-for-manifestation/

ReFaey, K., et al. (2019, May). The Eye of Horus: The Connection Between Art, Medicine, and Mythology in Ancient Egypt. Cureus, 11(5).

Reyes, P., et al. (2023). Physiology, Cellular Messengers. Treasure Island, FL: StatPearls Publishing.

Rizzi, M., et al. (2002). Structural Biology of Enzymes Involved in NAD and Molybdenum Cofactor Biosynthesis. Current Opinion in Structural Biology, 12(6).

Robbins, T. (1989). Unlimited power. New York, NY: Free Press.

Ryff, C.D., et al. (2001, May) Elective affinities and uninvited agonies: Mapping emotion with significant others onto health. In: Ryff, C.D., et al. Emotion, social relationships, and health: Third annual Wisconsin symposium on emotion. Oxford University Press; New York: in press.

Saladin, K. (2011). Human Anatomy (3rd ed.). McGraw-Hill.

Sancier, K.M. (1996, January). Medical Applications of Qigong. Alternative Therapies, 2(1).

Sara, S.J., Segal, M. (1991). Plasticity of sensory responses of locus coeruleus neurons in the behaving rat. Implications for cognition. Progress in Brain Research, 88.

Sarkar, S., et al. (2023, February 9). Efficacy of information transmission in cellular communication. Physical Review Research, 5.

Schnitzler, A., & Gross, J. (2005). Normal and Pathological Oscillatory Communication in the Brain. Nature Reviews Neuroscience, 6(4).

Scholem, G.G. (1961). Major Trends in Jewish Mysticism. Schocken Books.

Schultes, R.E. (2001). Plants of the Gods: Their Sacred, Healing, and Hallucinogenic Powers. Healing Arts Press.

Schultz, M.B., et al. (2016). Why NAD+ Declines During Aging: It's Destroyed. Cell Metabolism, 23(6).

Schwartz, J., & Begley, S. (2002). The mind and the brain: Neuroplasticity and the power of mental force. New York: Regan Books.

Scott, E. (2024, January 30). Understanding the Law of Attraction. VeryWellMind, from: https://www.verywellmind.com/understanding-and-using-the-law-of-attraction-3144808#toc-the-laws-of-attraction

Silva, J. (1977). The Silva Mind Control Method. New York, NY: Pocket Books.

Silva, Lauren. (2023, September 4). What Is Neurofeedback Therapy? Forbes Health, from: https://www.forbes.com/health/mind/what-is-neurofeedback-therapy/

Sivin, N. (1988). Science and Medicine in Imperial China—The State of the Field. The Journal of Asian Studies, 47(1).

Sivin, N. (1993). Huang ti nei ching 黃帝內經. In Early Chinese Texts: A Bibliographical Guide, ed., by M.l Loewe. University of California Press.

Smith, B.A., Goldberg, N.R., Meshul, C.K. (2011). Effects of treadmill exercise on behavioral recovery and changes in the substantia nigra and striatum of the 1-methyl-4-phenyl-1,2,3,6-tetrahydropyridine-lesioned mouse. Brain Research, 1386.

Smith, J.D. (2009). The Mahābhārata: an abridged translation. Penguin Classics.

Smith, P. (2000). "Meditation". A concise encyclopedia of the Baháʼí Faith. Oxford: Oneworld Publications.

Solomon, H. (2002, December 16). The self in transformation: the passage from a two- to a three-dimensional internal world. Journal of Analytical Psychology, 42(2).

Solomon, R.C; Higgins, K.M. (2003). From Africa to Zen: An Invitation to World Philosophy. Lanham, MD: Rowman & Littlefield.

Southgate, C. (2011). God, Humanity, and the Cosmos. New York, NY: T&T Clark International.

Sparkes, M. (2024, January 30). Neuralink: What do brain implants do and why is Elon Musk making them?. NewScientist, from: https://www.newscientist.com/article/2414852-neuralink-what-do-brain-implants-do-and-why-is-elon-musk-making-them/

Steiner, B., et al. (2006). Enriched environment induces cellular plasticity in the adult substantia nigra and improves motor function in the 6-OHDA rat model of Parkinson's Disease. Experimental Neurology, 199.

Sternheimer, J. (1984). Musique des particules élémentaires: invariance d'échelle, quantification et lois musicales dans la matière. Compte rendu du Collège de France.

Sternheimer, J. (1987). Musique des particules élémentaires. Le Cahier (Collège International de Philosophie).

Strassman, R. (2000) DMT: The Spirit Molecule: A Doctor's Revolutionary Research into the Biology of Near-Death and Mystical Experiences. Park Street Press.

Strogatz, S. (2003). Sync: How Order Emerges from Chaos in the Universe, Nature, and Daily Life. New York, NY: Hachette Books.

Subramanian, V.K. (1977). Saundaryalahari of Sankaracarya: Sanskrit Text in Devanagari with Roman Transliteration. Motilal Banarsidass Publishers Pvt. Ltd.

Sundarraj, M. (1994) "Ch. 4 Asvins—Time-Keepers". In Mahalingam, N. (ed.). RG Vedic Studies. Coimbatore: Rukmani Offset Press.

Suttie, J. (2018, October 24). Five Ways Mindfulness Meditation Is Good for Your Health. Greater Good Magazine: University of California, Berkeley, from: https://greatergood.berkeley.edu/article/item/five_ways_mindfulness_meditation_is_good_for_your_health

Swain, P. (2020). The Silva Method. BDJ Team, 7(7).

Swain R.A., Thompson R.F. (1993). In search of engrams. Annals of the New York Academy of Sciences, 702.

Swanson, C. (2003). The Synchronized Universe. Poseidia Press.

Tang, Y., et al. (2015, March 18). The neuroscience of mindfulness meditation. Nature Reviews Neuroscience, 16.

Taylor, T. (2010). The Science Behind the Secret: Decoding the Law of Attraction. Baen.

Tenenbaum, D. (2007, June 25). Research of Richard Davidson shows how meditation changes the mind. Waisman Center, University of Wisconsin-Madison, from: https://www.waisman.wisc.edu/2007/06/25/research-of-richard-davidson-shows-how-meditation-changes-the-mind/

Thaut, M.H., et al. (2015). Progress in Brain Research, Music, Neurology, and Neuroscience: Evolution, the Musical Brain, Medical Conditions, and Therapies. Elsevier.

Thompson, S.P. (1903, March 23). William Gilbert, and Terrestrial Magnetism in the Time of Queen Elizabeth [Discourse]. Meeting of the Royal Geographical Society, London, England.

Timalsina, S. (2017, May 24). Visualization in Hindu Practice. Oxford Research Encyclopedias: Religion.

Tinker, G. (2004). Spirit and Resistance: Political Theology and American Indian Liberation. Fortress Press.

Tolle, E. (2005). A new earth awakening to your life's purpose. New York, NY: A Plume Book.

Trafton, A. (2014). In the blink of an eye. Massachusetts Institute of Technology, from: https://news.mit.edu/2014/in-the-blink-of-an-eye-0116#:~:text=You%20might%20think%20it%20would,of%20-such%20rapid%20processing%20speed

Trapp J., et al. (2006). The Role of NAD+ Dependent Histone Deacetylases (sirtuins) in Ageing. Current Drug Targets, 7(11).

Ullo, M.F., et al. (2023, February 13). How cells sense and integrate information from different sources. WIREs Mechanisms of Disease, 15(4).

University Of Wisconsin-Madison. (2003, February 4).

University Of Wisconsin Study Reports Sustained Changes In Brain And Immune Function After Meditation. ScienceDaily, from: www.sciencedaily.com/releases/2003/02/030204074125.htm

Valls, C.O., et al. (2022, April). Signalling dynamics, cell decisions, and homeostatic control in health and disease. Current Opinion in Cell Biology, 75.

Vermin, M. (1977). The history and varieties of Jewish Meditation. Jason Aronson, Inc.

Vishnudevananda, S. (1988). The Complete Illustrated Book of Yoga. Harmony/Rodale.

von Bartheld, C.S., Bahney, J., & Herculano-Houzel, S. (2016). The Search for True Numbers of Neurons and Glial Cells in the Human Brain: A Review of 150 Years of Cell Counting. The Journal of Comparative Neurology, 524(18).

Walsh, R., et al. (2006). The meeting of meditative disciplines and western psychology: A mutually enriching dialogue. Psychologist, 61(3).

Wang, Y., et al. (2017, October 30). Positive Emotion Facilitates Cognitive Flexibility: An fMRI Study. Frontiers in Psychology, 8.

Ward, L.F. (1918). Glimpses of the Cosmos: Volume VI. G.P. Putnam's Sons.

Weinberger, N.M. (2004). Specific long-term memory traces in primary auditory cortex. Nature Reviews Neuroscience, 5.

Weingarten, C. P., et al. (2016). A new spin on neural processing: quantum cognition. Frontiers in Human Neuroscience, 10(541).

Weisskopf, V. (1981). The Development of Field Theory in the Last 50 Years. Physics Today, 34(11).

Wheeler, J.A., with Ford, K. (1998). Geons, Black Holes and Quantum Foam: A Life in Physics. W.W. Norton.

Whiting, R. (1991). Religions for Today. London: Stanley Thomas.

Wicker, B., et al. (2003). Both of us disgusted in my insula: The common neural basis of seeing and feeling disgust. Neuron, 40.

Wielgosz, J., et al. (2019, May 7). Mindfulness Meditation and Psychopathology. Annual Review of Clinical Psychology, 15.

Will, U., & Berg, E. (2007). Brain Wave Synchronization and Entrainment to Periodic Acoustic Stimuli. Neuroscience Letters, 424(1).

Winerman, L. (2012, September). Changing our brains, changing ourselves. American Psychological Association, Monitor on Psychology, 43(8).

Witchalls, C. (2015, February 9). Repairing the brain: Why we're living in an age of neuroscience. Independent, from: https://www.independent.co.uk/life-style/health-and-families/features/repairing-the-brain-why-we-re-living-in-an-age-of-neuroscience-10034606.html

Wurtman, R.J., Axelrod J (July 1965). The Pineal Gland. Scientific American, 213(1).

Yamboliev, I.A., et al. (2009). Storage and Secretion of Beta-NAD, ATP and Dopamine in NGF-Differentiated Rat Pheochromocytoma PC12 Cells. European Journal.

Yang, J-M. (1989). The root of Chinese Chi kung: the secrets of Chi kung training. Yang's Martial Arts Association.

Yin, J. (2019, April 23). Study on the Progress of Neural Mechanism of Positive Emotions. Translational Neuroscience, 10.

Zanzig, T. (1996). Christian Meditation for Beginners. Saint Mary's Press.

Zhang, G.S. (2017, November 3). Buddhism and the Law of Attraction: Musings over a Father's Writings to His Son in 1602. Buddhist Door Global, from: https://www.buddhistdoor.net/features/buddhism-and-the-law-of-attraction-musings-over-a-fathers-writings-to-his-son-in-1602/

Zysk, K. (1993). Religious Medicine: The History and Evolution of Indian Medicine. Routledge.

ALSO BY DAVID WONG

LIFE OF QI: THE SCIENCE OF LIFE FORCE

Discover the story and scientific research of a young man who self-healed from an incurable disease through Qi energy technology—explore his inventions, his inspiring transformation, and his vision for the future.

Get your copy at QiLifeStore.com!

"FASCINATING! David's depth of insight into the power of the mind is profound." — DR. PATRICK PORTER, PhD • Neuro Scientist & Inventor of Braintrap®

"David Wong is a MASTER OF ENERGY. He knows how to create it, control it, and project it." — DAVID LEE • Founder of TheBioHack.org

"David's story will INSPIRE you. With Qi, he fuses spirituality and science and brings insight and hope." — DR. JOY KONG, MD : Founder of Chara Biologics

EXPLORE MORE RESOURCES

CONTINUE YOUR LEARNING JOURNEY

Review This Book on Amazon: Help others by sharing your thoughts. Your feedback is invaluable. Visit **FrequencyReview.com**

Book a Free Product Consultation: Tailor your transformational journey with expert guidance. Visit **QiLifeAdvisor.com**

ENHANCE YOUR PRACTICE

Free 30-Day Qi Gong Challenge: Elevate your daily practices with guided exercises. Visit **DavidWongQiGong.com**

Abundance Workshop: Master wealth manifesting techniques in our interactive workshop. Visit **FrequencyDestiny.com**

DISCOVER FREQUENCY TECHNOLOGIES

Qi Coil™ Rife & P.E.M.F. Therapy: Discover the transformative benefits of Qi Coil™ therapy. Visit **QiLifeStore.com**

AUTOMATED QUANTUM HEALING & ABUNDANCE

Programming: Experience a 7-Day Free Trial of automated programming for wellness and prosperity. Visit **QiEnergy.Ai**

Free Quantum Frequencies: Access transformative frequencies at no cost. Visit **Members.QiCoil.com**

Abundance Frequencies: Begin attracting abundance with higher quantum frequencies. Visit **QiLifeStore.com/pages/abundance**

Ultimate Abundance Frequencies: Harness our most potent frequencies for wealth and prosperity. Visit **HiddenDragonClub.com**